Alyce Alexandra is the best-selling author of eight
thermo cooker cookbooks. She has her own range
of thermo cooker accessories, runs her own thermo
cooker cooking school and is creator of The TM Shop
and alycealexandra.com, selling all things
thermo cooker related.

Alyce is passionate about every avenue of food,
from seedling to stomach. Her mission is to get
people cooking, more often and from scratch, by
showing how easy, achievable and rewarding home
cooking can be. Her unpretentious, work-every-time
recipes have made her a much-loved figure in the
thermo cooker community. She lives, gardens, writes,
cooks and eats in Victoria, Australia.

www.alycealexandra.com
@alycealexandracookbooks

ALSO BY ALYCE ALEXANDRA

Quick Fix in the Thermomix

Miniseries: Low Carb

Quick Fix: Every Occasion

Miniseries: Super Healthy

Recipes from our Cooking School

Quick Dinners

Everyday Thermo Cooking

thermo cooker FRESH FAVOURITES

alyce alexandra

VIKING
an imprint of
PENGUIN BOOKS

This book is dedicated to my family:
Mum, Dad, Loryn and Ellen.

I am all that I am
because you are all that you are.

CONTENTS

AUTUMN

WINTER

WHAT'S IN THE FRIDGE?

INTRODUCTION

There's nothing I'm surer of than the importance of home cooking using real, fresh ingredients. The benefits to individuals, families, community, environment, farmers and animal welfare are vast, but in today's busy society cooking is often the first thing we outsource. While some may argue this makes economic sense, the cost and benefit of doing so cannot be measured in dollars alone. To my mind, the only way forward is to keep cooking easy and fuss-free, relying on simple and satisfying combinations of fresh ingredients that anyone can do at home. And that's exactly why I wrote *Thermo Cooker Fresh Favourites*.

This book is the food I eat at my table, the food I cook for my friends and family. And I hope this is the food that you enjoy and come to share with your loved ones also. This isn't an aspirational coffee table book, this is a real cookbook, a helping hand to be your partner in the kitchen. These are achievable recipes, made without fancy techniques or dexterity. I don't profess to create Heston masterpieces or have cheffy skills, and nor would I want to. Who

better to understand the desires and limitations of the home cook than the home cook herself? Life is complicated enough – cooking doesn't have to be.

While I certainly don't believe a thermo cooker is essential to cooking delicious and nutritious food, boy, it makes it quicker, easier and vastly more enjoyable! In turn, I can cook more than I ever could without it, in a whole lot less time. I truly believe that, regardless of skill level or time constraints, anyone with a thermo cooker can cook nourishing and delicious food they are proud to serve and share. And that excites me! For there is so much to be gained, and in today's busy world we could all do with a little help.

Fresh cooking is a celebration of produce, centering the dish on whatever's at its seasonal best. It's about real ingredients – foods that cultures have relied on for years that don't necessitate long ingredient lists. Fresh is uncomplicated, because quality ingredients brought together simply is all you need. For me, cooking almost always starts with the produce itself – how to make the most of my

heirloom tomatoes straight from the garden, a beautiful peach from the market or the leftover bits and pieces in the veggie drawer. That's why I've made fresh produce the heart of this cookbook, celebrating all that nature has to offer.

I may be all about fresh, but boy am I all about flavour! No rabbit food in this cookbook. I've got pizzas, pastas, curries, cakes, sorbets, soups, salads, breads, burgers, bagels, dips, drinks, dumplings, tarts and more, all with fresh twists and all sure to satisfy. I've got recipes to cover you for breakfast, lunch, dinner, dessert and everything in between, 365 days of the year. Included are freezer friendly meals, hearty dinners, fermenting recipes, baked goods, ways to use up leftovers, snacks for on the go, preserving recipes, refreshing sweet treats, warming breakfasts and much, much more. All the sections of this book contain a diverse range of dishes – some perfect to whip up quickly mid-week, others a little more special. Having a mix of recipes that need to be prepared on the spot and recipes that can be made in advance is important to me. When you've got

a little extra time you can prepare and stockpile, and when you don't, you're still only 15 or 20 minutes from something delicious and nutritious. Many recipes cater to a wide variety of dietary requirements, including vegetarian, vegan, dairy free, gluten free, nut free and refined-sugar free, with others containing variations to adapt to such preferences.

I've loosely themed this book and the recipes in it into the four seasons – the freshest and best produce is always going to be what's in season, so to me a fresh cookbook evokes a seasonal motif. But by no means are you limited to only a quarter of the book at any one time! Most recipes span over multiple seasons, and some across the whole year. It's merely a way for you to start thinking about fresh produce and connecting with your food. I've also included my 'what's in the fridge' recipe guides that transcend seasons and shopping lists, showing you how to make a delicious and nutritious meal using only what you've already got in the pantry and fridge. Not sure what's in season in your area? I've included seasonal lists throughout this book,

but your best bet is to head to a farmers market – whatever people are selling in abundance is what's going to be at its seasonal peak and freshest. If you're shopping in a supermarket, look for produce grown in your home country, and usually whatever's at its seasonal best is also at its cheapest (which is convenient!).

And with that, I pass the baton to you. To cook these recipes, to draw inspiration from my ideas and to ultimately make them your own, for you and your family to enjoy. To cook more often, cook from scratch and become a more proficient thermo cook along the way. For this book is only as successful as the oil spatters and grubby fingerprints it is marked with, and the smiles it brings.

Lots of love from my kitchen to yours,

alyce xo

THE BASICS

- **OIL** I use extra virgin olive oil for all raw applications and in the thermo cooker to temperatures up to and including 100°C. For anything hotter than that, such as on the stove and in the oven, I use macadamia or coconut oil as they have a higher smoke point. There are many great quality and ethical brands of all three.

- **SALT** I recommend using a good-quality, pure, unrefined salt. Salt is not simply for saltiness; it acts as an enhancer, highlighting all the flavours in the dish. If something tastes bland, it probably needs a little salt. Often it is fine to add salt to taste, but if an exact measure is specified I will always indicate the type of salt used. This is important as one teaspoon of fine salt is saltier than one teaspoon of coarse salt or flakes! I recommend always using fine salt for baking, but for general seasoning salt flakes are delicious.

- **FLOUR** For the best bread it is essential to use baker's flour, also known as bread flour or strong flour. This has more gluten than regular plain flour, and therefore more protein. As a general rule, 9–10% protein content is a soft flour ideal for cakes, whereas 12–14% protein is a stronger flour ideal for bread.

- **EGGS** Always free range. But not all free range is equal, with stocking densities and other policies fluctuating dramatically between brands. Check the rules of the individual certifying bodies, and if in doubt price is usually a good indicator of quality. Many good brands are now including outdoor stocking densities on the carton – look for 1500 birds per hectare or fewer.

- **DAIRY** I always use full-fat dairy products, not only because I like to cook with unrefined ingredients wherever possible, but simply because they taste better! Low-fat products just don't cut it in my book (pardon the pun!).

- **FRUIT AND VEGETABLES** While organic is great where possible, I believe that buying local, seasonal produce is just as important. Shop at farmers markets and browse online for co-ops – some of them even do home delivery. Better yet, grow some of your own! Herbs, rocket, zucchini and tomatoes would be my pick to start.

- **BEEF** Where possible I cook with beef that is locally grown, grass fed and finished. To me, it doesn't make sense to grow food to feed food. Buying meat directly from the farmer is a great way to get quality products at reasonable prices and you have a much better chance of knowing how the animal lived, and how it died. Don't be afraid to ask questions; people who care will be happy to share the answers.

- **SEAFOOD** My preferred seafood picks are always the most sustainable ones, such as oysters, mussels, sardines, mackerel, whiting, bream, crab, calamari, squid and octopus. Buy local wherever possible, and diversify your choices to spread the impact of fishing pressures.

- **WEIGHTS** The weight specified for each ingredient is the weight after the ingredient has been prepared per instruction (for example, pumpkin, peeled, seeds removed). Please factor this in when shopping.

- **TEASPOONS** I use Australian metric measurements, meaning 1 teaspoon = 5 ml and 1 tablespoon = 20ml.

- **OVEN** All oven temperatures are for a fan-forced setting, unless otherwise stated. My experience is that oven temperatures can vary dramatically, so I recommend you get to know your own oven and adjust the temperatures accordingly. You may also need to rotate baking trays during the cooking time to ensure even cooking and browning.

DIETARY REQUIREMENTS

For recipes catering for specific dietary requirements look for the following:

—— DAIRY FREE
Dairy free

—— DAIRY-FREE (OPTION)
Follow the variation for a dairy-free option

—— GLUTEN FREE*
Gluten free

—— GLUTEN-FREE* (OPTION)
Follow the variation for a gluten-free option

—— VEGETARIAN
Vegetarian

—— VEGETARIAN (OPTION)
Follow the variation for a vegetarian option

—— VEGAN
Vegan

—— VEGAN (OPTION)
Follow the variation for a vegan option

—— QUICK FIX
The entire recipe can be completed and on the table in less than 30 minutes

—— QUICK FIX +
The total hands-on time is less than 30 minutes, but the recipe also requires baking, marinating, soaking, proving, chilling or freezing time, as indicated.

* While every effort has been made to indicate gluten-free ingredients, make sure you read the ingredients list of all food products to ensure they are suitable for a gluten-free diet.

THERMO COOKERS AND TERMINOLOGY

The recipes in this cookbook have been developed and tested in the Thermomix TM31 and Thermomix TM5 models; however, they are suitable for use across many thermo cookers, including:

- Thermomix TM5
- Thermomix TM31
- Thermochef Natura
- BioChef MyCook
- Optimum ThermoCook
- Intelli Kitchen Master
- Supercook

- HotmixPRO
- SuperChef
- ThermoPro
- ThermoBlend
- Mistral Professional Ultimate Kitchen Machine

Some recipes will also be suitable for high-speed food processors and blenders.

It is natural to expect some variation between brands of thermo cooker, and slight adaptations to the method may be required, depending on your machine.

TERMINOLOGY

TC: Thermo cooker

MC: Measuring cup that sits in the top of the thermo cooker lid

STEAMING TEMPERATURE: Many machines have a special steaming function (in the Thermomix this is called Varoma temperature), but if yours doesn't, use 110°C

STEAMING BASKET: This basket sits inside the thermo cooker bowl and needs to be inserted before securing the lid

STEAMING TRAY: This attachment sits on top of the thermo cooker bowl and needs to be placed on top after securing the lid

DOUGH FUNCTION: Many machines have a special dough function (in the Thermomix this is called interval speed), but if not, start at speed 6 for 10–20 seconds, then drop to a lower speed until a dough is formed

ASSISTING WITH SPATULA: This requires you to put the spatula in the hole in the lid and stir while the thermo cooker is in operation

SPRING

The longer days and long-forgotten rays of sunshine energise and regenerate. I love how the garden comes back to life in spectacular fashion with brightly coloured tulips and daffodils, announcing the warm weather is coming, even if we can't feel it just yet! Meals shift from heavier dishes to lighter takes, making the most of the fresh new produce. Newfound energy makes this the perfect time to cook investment flavour makers – recipes that will reap rewards for months to come. It's also a great time to try something new, such as fermenting, giving both your health and tastebuds a boost.

My favourite spring produce:

Asparagus	Grapefruit
Basil	Kale
Beans	Lemon
Beetroot	Lime
Cabbage	Onion
Cauliflower	Peas
Coriander	Radish
Cucumber	Spinach
Garlic	Zucchini

fresh and light

A collection of meals on the lighter side using bold
flavours and vibrant ingredients, these dishes will leave
you satisfied and content – by no means am I talking rabbit
food! I've got pastas, soups, salads, pizzas and pastries all
centered around fresh ingredients, and all easily prepared.
Most make delicious lunchbox options, so relish the
leftovers and enjoy again the next day.

This soup is a really handy addition to my quick-fix repertoire, and despite its simplicity it is bursting with flavour, thanks to the curry paste. While I usually find homemade pastes far superior to what you can find in a jar at the supermarket, at a pinch I would happily turn to the latter. Zucchinis are plentiful right throughout spring, summer and autumn, and, in my experience anyway, are the easiest vegetable to grow – so why don't you pop a seedling in this spring?

THAI ZUCCHINI SOUP

1 brown onion, peeled and
    halved
2 garlic cloves, peeled
3cm piece ginger, peeled
80g green curry paste (see
    page 161)
20g coconut oil
500g zucchini, roughly
    chopped
500g water
400g can coconut milk
50g stock concentrate (see
    page 249)
50g spinach leaves
Fried shallots, to serve

SERVES 4

DAIRY FREE
GLUTEN FREE
VEGETARIAN
VEGAN

QUICK FIX

1. Place onion, garlic and ginger in TC bowl, chop for 5 seconds, speed 5. Scrape down sides.
2. Add curry paste and coconut oil, sauté 5 minutes, 100°C, speed 1.
3. Add zucchini, water, coconut milk and stock concentrate, cook for 12 minutes, 100°C, speed 2.
4. Add spinach leaves, purée for 1 minute, slowly increasing to speed 9.

TO SERVE

Divide between 4 serving bowls and top with fried shallots and some fresh herbs if you've got them on hand. A piece of roti bread complements perfectly and adds an Asian twist to the usual side of toast.

NOTE

For a vegetarian and vegan meal ensure your curry paste is vegan, as they can contain fish products. (Our recipe on page 161 doesn't!)

I've always been put off cooking falafels at home due to the amount of oil required to deep or shallow fry them, but I've found a shortcut! Fry them in a standard amount of oil, just like a meatball, then finish the cooking in the oven. This way, I've found, you get that crispy crunchy fried outer and a light and moist cooked centre. The mixture itself is so easy to make, but you must must must remember to soak the chickpeas 24 hours in advance!

FALAFELS

300g dried chickpeas soaked for 24 hours in plenty of water, drained
2 teaspoons coriander seeds
3 teaspoons cumin seeds
5 garlic cloves, peeled
1 brown onion, peeled and halved
Handful fresh parsley, leaves only
Handful fresh mint, leaves only
2 teaspoons sweet paprika
2 teaspoons fine salt
1 pinch ground cardamom
1 teaspoon bicarbonate of soda
50g plain flour
Oil, for frying (macadamia or grapeseed)

MAKES 20 FALAFELS

DAIRY FREE
GLUTEN FREE (OPTION)
VEGETARIAN
VEGAN

1. Preheat oven to 160°C.
2. Place coriander and cumin seeds in TC bowl, mill for 20 seconds, speed 10.
3. Add drained chickpeas, garlic, onion, parsley, mint, paprika, salt, cardamom and bicarbonate of soda, chop for 10 seconds, speed 5. Scrape down sides.
4. Add flour, mix for 6 seconds, speed 4, or until flour is combined.
5. Heat a liberal amount of oil in a large fry pan over medium heat – use enough oil to completely cover the base.
6. Use wet hands to form walnut-size balls of falafel mixture and add as many as will fit without crowding to the hot oil. Cook for 8 minutes or until golden, turning every 2–3 minutes to ensure even cooking. Place on a baking tray and transfer to the oven for 10–15 minutes (this is essential to ensure the falafels are cooked through and to keep them warm while cooking the second batch). Repeat with remaining falafels.

TO SERVE

Serve in pita bread or a lettuce cup (pictured) with salad and tzatziki, hummus or garlic sauce. You can also refrigerate cooked falafels and reheat in the oven at 160°C before serving.

NOTE

If mixture is too wet to form into balls, add a tablespoon of flour and fold through to combine – this will stiffen the mixture slightly.

VARIATION

For a gluten-free option, use a gluten-free flour.

You might be a little dubious about this recipe – I know I was when Ellen first suggested it! But I promise you'll be pleasantly surprised by how impressive these healthy cauliflower bases are. They have a crispy bottom just like their traditional wheat counterparts, meaning you can safely pick them up and eat with your fingers – just how pizza should be enjoyed, no knife and fork required!

CAULIFLOWER PIZZA BASES

4 garlic cloves, peeled
500g cauliflower, florets and
    stems roughly chopped
1 teaspoon fine salt
3 teaspoons dried oregano
250g buckwheat flour
20g macadamia oil

Toppings – tomato passata,
    pesto, tomatoes, roasted
    eggplant, roasted
    mushrooms, spinach,
    olives, grated cheese,
    roast pumpkin, pine nuts,
    marinated artichoke,
    roasted capsicum, chilli,
    zucchini, onion

SERVES 3

DAIRY FREE
GLUTEN FREE
VEGETARIAN
VEGAN

1. Preheat oven to 170°C. Line a large pizza stone or baking tray with a baking mat or baking paper.

2. Place garlic in TC bowl, chop for 5 seconds, speed 6.

3. Add cauliflower, salt and oregano, chop for 5 seconds, speed 7, or until you have fine crumbs. Scrape down sides.

4. Add flour and oil, mix for 10 seconds, speed 4. Fold in any remaining flour using a spatula.

5. Divide mixture into 6 and place on prepared tray, pressing out to a thickness of 4mm. Bake for 25 minutes, or until golden and crisp around the edges.

6. Add toppings, return to oven for 10 minutes, or until toppings are warmed through.

TO SERVE

Enjoy hot out of the oven with a drizzle of olive oil or chilli oil (see page 37).

I will admit this recipe is a little fiddlier than most of mine, but I really think the result is worth it – every time I eat one I am pleasantly surprised, which says a lot as I am always my own harshest critic! They're also delicious cold, so I relish any leftovers. While pastry may not have been the obvious choice for the 'fresh and light' section, the filo really does give a lightness and the dill a freshness – you might be surprised too.

SPANAKOPITA CIGARS

400g spinach leaves

2 spring onions, ends trimmed
    and halved

2 red Asian shallots, peeled

1 leek, white part only,
    quartered

30g olive oil

Handful fresh dill

200g Greek feta, roughly
    crumbled

2 free-range eggs

Salt, to taste

12 sheets filo pastry

2 tablespoons melted butter

Sesame seeds (optional)

SERVES 4

VEGETARIAN

1. Place half the spinach in TC bowl, chop for 5 seconds, speed 5, assisting with spatula. Set aside.

2. Place remaining spinach in TC bowl, chop for 5 seconds, speed 5.

3. Return reserved spinach to TC bowl and cook the entire amount for 5 minutes, 100°C, speed 2. Transfer to TC steamer basket and allow to drain excess liquid.

4. Place spring onions, shallots and leek in dry TC bowl, chop for 5 seconds, speed 5. Scrape down sides.

5. Add oil, sauté for 5 minutes, 100°C, speed 1.

6. Add dill, feta, eggs and salt, mix for 5 seconds, speed 4. Add drained spinach and combine using spatula. Refrigerate for a minimum of 30 minutes.

7. Preheat oven to 200°C.

8. Lay 1 sheet of pastry flat and brush sparingly with melted butter. Top with a second sheet of pastry. Brush again with melted butter and top with a third sheet of pastry. Place a quarter of the spinach mixture along the bottom of the long end of the pastry, leaving a 10cm border on each of the short sides. Fold the short sides inwards to partially cover the spinach mixture and then carefully roll up like a cigar keeping the mixture tightly packed inside. Brush melted butter along the exposed edge to form a seal. Repeat with remaining pastry and filling to form 4 spanakopita cigars. Brush tops with any remaining butter and sprinkle with sesame seeds if using.

9. Place on a lined baking tray and bake for 20 minutes, or until pastry is golden.

TO SERVE

Serve with a Greek salad or dressed mesclun mix.
A tomato chutney is the obvious condiment pick,
but any savoury relish works.

I fell in love with these oysters at one of my family's favourite restaurants, Longrain, as they are the perfect balance of spicy, salty, sweet and sour. I am always looking for new ways to enjoy these little delicacies as they are one of the most sustainable seafood options – filtering the sea water and requiring no additional feed. Of course, I had to try to replicate the dish at home, and given how dead easy it turned out to be, I'm very glad I did.

THAI CHILLI OYSTERS

2 long red chillies

2 bird's eye chillies

1 garlic clove, peeled

2 coriander stalks, roots and
leaves

1 lime, juice only

30g coconut sugar

20g rice vinegar

½ teaspoon fine salt

24 freshly shucked oysters

Fried shallots, to serve

MAKES 24

DAIRY FREE
GLUTEN FREE

QUICK FIX

1. Place chillies, garlic, coriander stalks and roots in TC bowl, chop for 3 seconds, speed 6. Scrape down sides.

2. Add lime juice, coconut sugar, rice vinegar and salt, mix for 5 seconds, speed 3. Refrigerate until ready to serve.

TO SERVE

Serve oysters drizzled with 1 teaspoon of sauce and topped with fried shallots and coriander leaves.

Simple yet satisfying, this dish is bound to become a family favourite! Especially when you realise how easy it is to make. Everything is done in the thermo cooker, including cooking the pasta – no stove required – and just a thermo bowl and a chopping board to wash up! I love the fresh combination of tomatoes, basil and olives, and what better way to bring them all together than with silky spaghetti?

ONE–BOWL TOMATO SPAGHETTI

1 brown onion, peeled and halved

1 long red chilli (optional)

3 garlic cloves, peeled

80g olive oil

150g black olives, pitted

550g ripe tomatoes, roughly diced

650g water

50g stock concentrate (see page 249)

10g balsamic vinegar

1½ teaspoons fine salt

400g spaghetti

Handful fresh basil, leaves picked, to serve

SERVES 4

DAIRY FREE
VEGETARIAN
VEGAN

1. Place onion, chilli and garlic in TC bowl, chop for 5 seconds, speed 5. Scrape down sides.

2. Add oil, sauté for 5 minutes, 100°C, speed 1.

3. Add olives, chop for 2 seconds, speed 6.

4. Add tomatoes, water, stock concentrate, balsamic vinegar and salt, cook for 8 minutes, 100°C, reverse speed soft.

5. Remove MC and add spaghetti through hole in lid. Cook for 4 minutes, 100°C, reverse speed soft.

6. Remove lid and submerge spaghetti into sauce using spatula. Replace lid and MC. Cook for 2 minutes, 100°C, reverse speed soft.

7. Gently stir spaghetti, folding the top spaghetti to the bottom. Replace lid and leave standing for 15 minutes in the TC bowl to complete cooking.

TO SERVE

Toss spaghetti with basil leaves. Optional extra toppings: try chilli flakes, toasted pine nuts, cherry tomatoes, rocket or grated cheese.

Smoked almonds
are an easy way
to add flavour.

This pasta tastes wayyyyy too good to be vegan, gluten free and loaded with kale! It's a real people pleaser, making it perfect for picnics or other 'bring a plate' get togethers. I usually enjoy it as a meal on its own, but it could just as easily serve as a delicious pasta side salad. The kale pesto sauce gives a fresh tang, while the currants add the perfect hint of sweetness. And don't worry, no one will be able to tell that it's buckwheat pasta!

SPRING GREEN PASTA

500g buckwheat spiral pasta
200g peas, fresh or frozen
150g smoked almonds
3 garlic cloves, peeled
50g black kale, spines removed
100g olive oil
1 lemon, juice only
60g apple cider vinegar
2 teaspoons fine salt
1 cucumber, cubed
2 spring onions, finely sliced
100g currants

SERVES 5

DAIRY FREE
GLUTEN FREE
VEGETARIAN
VEGAN

QUICK FIX

1. Cook pasta on stove according to packet instructions. Two minutes before pasta is cooked, add peas. Drain peas and pasta.

2. Meanwhile, place almonds in TC bowl, chop for 2 seconds, speed 6. Remove almonds from TC bowl and set aside.

3. Without cleaning TC bowl, add garlic and kale, chop for 5 seconds, speed 6. Scrape down sides.

4. Add 20g oil, sauté for 7 minutes, 100°C, speed 1.5.

5. Add remaining 80g oil, lemon juice, vinegar and salt, purée for 10 seconds, speed 9.

6. Toss kale dressing with pasta, peas, chopped almonds, cucumber, spring onions and currants.

TO SERVE
Serve immediately or refrigerate and enjoy cold later. Great packed in containers for easy meals on the go.

NOTE
Smoked almonds work brilliantly in this dish but can be substituted with roasted almonds.

No one will believe the beef has been steamed!

As strange as it sounds, one of my favourite ways to cook beef is to steam it in the thermo steaming tray. It is such a gentle and foolproof way to cook – I promise you can't dry the meat out! By slicing it as thinly as possible, no one will notice that it's missing the usual brown exterior. Toss with the vibrant fresh ingredients and the delicious miso-sesame-honey dressing and, in the words of Jamie – happy days!

SPRING SALAD WITH MISO DRESSING

1 litre water

500g piece trimmed grass-fed rump steak

2 bunches thick asparagus, bottoms trimmed

70g white miso paste

60g hulled tahini

40g apple cider vinegar

40g honey

30g olive oil

1 bunch baby radishes, thinly sliced

1 bunch fresh mint, leaves picked

120g salad greens

Toasted sesame seeds, to garnish

SERVES 4

DAIRY FREE
GLUTEN FREE

QUICK FIX

1. Fill TC bowl with the water. Place beef on lower steaming tray and asparagus on upper steaming tray. Steam for 17 minutes, steaming temperature, speed 3.

2. Remove asparagus and check beef is cooked to your liking (it will be rare at this stage). If not, continue cooking beef for a further 3 minutes, steaming temperature, speed 3. Check again. Once cooked, set aside to rest.

3. In a clean TC bowl, place miso, tahini, vinegar, honey and oil, mix for 20 seconds, speed 4.

TO SERVE

Slice beef as thinly as possible using a sharp knife, then toss with asparagus, radishes, mint and salad greens. Drizzle with miso dressing, sprinkle with toasted sesame seeds and serve.

I love the freshness and pretty hue of pomegranate arils.

Super easy, all you'll need for this meal is your thermo bowl, knife, chopping board and 25 minutes (20 of those you can be off doing something else!). This is speedy, simple and satisfying mid-week fare with a good dose of veggies – bowl food at its best, possibly eaten on the couch.

RAINBOW RICE

1 brown onion, peeled and halved
20g olive oil
2 carrots, peeled and quartered
400g basmati rice, rinsed just prior to cooking
200g peas, fresh or frozen
1 red capsicum, diced
720g water
60g stock concentrate (see page 249)
1 teaspoon ground turmeric
½ teaspoon ground cumin
100g currants
1 cucumber, cubed
40g flaked almonds, toasted
Handful mint leaves, finely chopped

SERVES 6

DAIRY FREE
GLUTEN FREE
VEGETARIAN
VEGAN

QUICK FIX

1. Place onion in TC bowl, chop for 5 seconds, speed 5. Scrape down sides.
2. Add oil, sauté for 5 minutes, 100°C, speed 1.
3. Add carrots, chop for 3 seconds, speed 5, or until grated.
4. Add rice, peas, capsicum, water and stock concentrate, cook for 11 minutes, 100°C, reverse speed 1.
5. Add turmeric, cumin and currants and fold through using spatula. Allow to sit in TC bowl for a minimum of 10 minutes before serving.

TO SERVE
Toss with cucumber, almonds and mint leaves. Optional extras – yoghurt, feta cheese or pomegranate arils (pictured). Delicious served warm or cold.

NOTE
This dish also makes an impressive side dish to curries.

This is about as fresh a dish as you'll find – a poke bowl with a base not of rice, but of raw broccoli! I agree raw broccoli isn't particularly appealing, which is why I've grated it up with Japanese flavours, making it sweet, spicy and tangy, while also slightly pickling it. The end result is surprisingly satisfying! Perfect for anyone wanting to lower the carb or calorie count of their meal, or anyone simply wanting to eat more veggies.

BROCCOLI POKE BOWL

1 long red chilli
30g pickled ginger
80g mirin
2 heads broccoli, cut into florets
    and stalks roughly chopped
80g white miso paste
80g apple cider vinegar
40g toasted sesame oil
40g maple syrup
40g tamari

Toppings – avocado, red
    cabbage, cucumber, carrot,
    steamed edamame beans,
    radish, fried kale, spring
    onion, boiled egg, fried tofu,
    mint, coriander, corn
    kernels, sautéed
    mushrooms, celery
Sesame seeds, to garnish

SERVES 4

DAIRY FREE
GLUTEN FREE
VEGETARIAN
VEGAN (OPTION)

QUICK FIX

1. Place chilli in TC bowl, chop for 3 seconds, speed 6. Scrape down sides.

2. Add ginger and 40g mirin, chop for 1 second, speed 9.

3. Add broccoli stalks, chop for 2 seconds, speed 5.

4. Add broccoli florets, chop for 4 seconds, speed 4, or until finely chopped, assisting with spatula. Remove from TC bowl and set aside.

5. In a clean TC bowl, place miso paste, apple cider vinegar, remaining 40g mirin, toasted sesame oil, maple syrup and tamari. Mix for 10 seconds, speed 4.

TO SERVE

Divide broccoli mixture between 4 serving bowls, add toppings, drizzle with miso dressing and sprinkle with sesame seeds.

My beautiful
mum Janene.

spruce it up

My top secret for quick and delicious home cooking is
to have an arsenal of flavour makers up your sleeve –
premade concoctions that you can use to 'spruce up' just
about any dish in no time at all. That way, no matter what
you've got in the fridge, you can whip something up that is
sure to satisfy. These are investment recipes, to make when
you've got a little extra time on your hands – and reaping
the rewards for months to come. I've included quick meal
suggestions to guide you for each, so you can see the
variety of delicious options these flavour makers create.

Dukkah is such a versatile condiment – you'll find me sprinkling it on everything! It has a salty, flavoursome richness that instantly adds excitement to salads and vegetables, making even the most mundane of dishes that little bit fancy. Speaking of fancy, don't forget dukkah's classic use – served with olive oil and crusty bread. Such an easy starter, yet one that is sure to have guests singing your praises.

CLASSIC DUKKAH

80g sesame seeds
100g macadamia nuts
75g blanched almonds
3 teaspoons coriander seeds
3 teaspoons cumin seeds
1½ teaspoons fine salt

MAKES 2 CUPS

DAIRY FREE
GLUTEN FREE
VEGETARIAN
VEGAN

QUICK FIX

1. Preheat oven to 170°C.
2. Spread sesame seeds, macadamia nuts and almonds evenly over a baking tray. Roast for 10 minutes, or until golden. Remove from oven and allow to cool for at least 10 minutes.
3. Meanwhile, place coriander seeds, cumin seeds and salt in TC bowl, mill for 10 seconds, speed 9.
4. Add nuts and seeds, mill for 4 seconds, speed 6, or until fine crumbs are formed.

STORAGE

Store in an airtight container in the fridge for up to 6 months.

SPRUCE IT UP

Brunch: Toast + eggs + asparagus + dukkah

Satisfying salad: Roasted veggies + salad greens + balsamic + olive oil + dukkah

Quick dinner: Cooked pasta + rocket + tomatoes + olives + feta + olive oil + dukkah

My favourite ways to serve dukkah.

This brilliantly hued oil pairs perfectly with Asian dishes, but its uses certainly don't end there! Despite the firey name, this oil is much more complex than just spicy heat, with chints of garlic, ginger, curry and citrus. Drizzle it wherever you would use a finishing splash of oil, such as on soups or pizzas (pictured) as we have done – it will instantly add flavour and excitement.

CHILLI OIL

2 red Asian shallots, peeled
3 garlic cloves, peeled
3cm piece ginger, peeled
3 small red chillies
1 star anise
250g rice bran oil
2 teaspoons curry powder
½ teaspoon hot chilli powder
    (optional)
½ lemon, rind only

MAKES 1 CUP

DAIRY FREE
GLUTEN FREE
VEGETARIAN
VEGAN

1. Place shallots, garlic, ginger, chilli and star anise in TC bowl, chop for 3 seconds, speed 6. Scrape down sides.
2. Add oil, curry powder, chilli powder (if using) and lemon rind, cook for 30 minutes, 90°C, speed 2. Allow to cool completely.
3. Strain oil through a fine sieve and refrigerate until ready to serve.

STORAGE
Store in the fridge for up to 1 month.

NOTE
You can use olive oil for this recipe but it will solidify in the fridge – simply leave it at room temperature for 30 minutes before using, to liquify.

SPRUCE IT UP
Breakfast: Scrambled eggs + toast + chilli oil

Simple side: Cooked white rice + sesame seeds + chilli oil

Bowl food: Cooked noodles + stir-fried veggies + fried shallots + chilli oil

My last book included a savoury seed sprinkle that was just so popular that I couldn't resist adapting it for sweet uses! The seeds are surprisingly satiating, adding an easy hit of protein to breakfasts and snacks alike, while the maple syrup satisfies the sweet tooth.

SWEET SEED SPRINKLES

50g coconut oil
80g maple syrup
100g coconut flakes
100g pumpkin seeds
100g sunflower seeds
50g sesame seeds
2 teaspoons ground cinnamon
Pinch fine salt

MAKES 4 CUPS

DAIRY FREE
GLUTEN FREE
VEGETARIAN
VEGAN

QUICK FIX + COOLING

1. Preheat oven to 140°C.
2. Place all ingredients in TC bowl, warm for 2 minutes, 50°C, reverse speed 1. Spread mixture over 2 large lined baking trays.
3. Bake for 10 minutes, then turn off oven. Allow mixture to cool completely inside the oven – do not open oven during this time.

STORAGE

Once cooled, transfer to an airtight jar or container and store for up to 1 month.

SPRUCE IT UP

Breakfast parfait: Yoghurt + fruit + seed sprinkles

Healthy dessert: Easy ice-cream (page 93) + seed sprinkles

Simple snack: Seed sprinkles!

This garlicky goodness is such an easy way to add flavour and texture to a multitude of meals. Next time you end up with bread that's going stale, slice it up and get it in the freezer! It will make the best breadcrumbs, and the best garlic crumbs. No need to go out and buy a fresh loaf – save that for smothering in homemade apricot jam!

GARLIC CRUMBS

6 garlic cloves, peeled
150g good-quality bread, frozen
      and roughly chopped
Handful fresh thyme sprigs,
      leaves picked
1½ teaspoons fine salt
20g macadamia oil

MAKES 2 CUPS

DAIRY FREE
VEGETARIAN
VEGAN

QUICK FIX

1. Preheat oven to 180°C.
2. Place garlic, bread, thyme and salt in TC bowl, chop for 10 seconds, speed 8, or until chunky breadcrumbs are formed.
3. Add oil, mix for 5 seconds, reverse speed 4.
4. Spread out evenly over a lined baking tray. Bake for 8 minutes, then stir to ensure even browning. Bake for a further 4 minutes, or until golden.

STORAGE

Allow to cool completely before storing in an airtight container for up to 1 month.

SPRUCE IT UP

Easy entertaining: Fresh oysters + garlic crumbs

Satisfying side: Roast pumpkin + garlic crumbs

Quick dinner: Spaghetti + rocket + olive oil + garlic crumbs

Look for extra virgin olive oil pressed locally and recently.

This buttery dip is rich and luxurious, but still fresh – thanks to the garlic and the peppery flavour of a good quality extra virgin olive oil. Use it wherever you would usually use cream cheese or mayonnaise, or as a standard dip. The fact it contains no dairy, eggs or vegetable oil makes it even the more versatile. You'll have to trust me with this recipe – granted it seems a little strange, but I promise the results are foolproof!

ALMOND AND GARLIC SPREAD

200g blanched almonds
2 garlic cloves, peeled
500g water
100g ice cubes
200g extra virgin olive oil
2 teaspoons sherry vinegar
1½ teaspoons fine salt

MAKES 2 CUPS

DAIRY FREE
GLUTEN FREE
VEGETARIAN
VEGAN

QUICK FIX

1. Place almonds, garlic and water in TC bowl, heat for 6 minutes, 100°C, reverse speed 1. Drain almonds and garlic through TC steamer basket or fine sieve, discarding water.
2. Place drained almonds and garlic back in TC bowl, add ice cubes, olive oil, sherry vinegar and salt. Purée for 1 minute, speed 9, or until smooth.

STORAGE

Transfer to a glass jar and store in the fridge for up to 2 weeks.

SPRUCE IT UP

Bagel breaky: Bagel + smoked salmon + lettuce + almond and garlic spread

Tasty tart: Shortcrust pastry tart shell + roasted veggies + almond and garlic spread

Satisfying snack: Vegetable crudités + almond and garlic spread

I'm always amazed by how thick and creamy this aioli is.

My sister Loryn developed this recipe to combat her aioli cravings, and it is such a winner! You'd never know that it didn't contain the usual egg yolk. This is a really handy recipe to have up your sleeve – between allergies, eating preferences and school rules, there seem to be more and more occasions when eggs are off the menu. I also love that there is no potential wastage of a precious egg white – I avoid splitting eggs wherever I can for this reason.

EGG-FREE AIOLI

1 garlic clove, peeled
100g soy milk
20g apple cider vinegar
20g Dijon mustard
¼ teaspoon fine salt
200g grapeseed oil

MAKES 1 CUP

DAIRY FREE
GLUTEN FREE
VEGETARIAN
VEGAN

QUICK FIX

1. Place garlic in TC bowl, chop for 5 seconds, speed 5.
2. Insert butterfly into TC bowl. Add soy milk, vinegar, mustard and salt. Mix for 4 seconds, speed 4.
3. Set timer for 1 minute, speed 4, while slowly drizzling oil through the hole in the lid.

STORAGE

Refrigerate until ready to serve as aioli will continue to thicken while it cools.

VARIATION

For a standard mayonnaise, omit garlic and follow the same steps with remaining ingredients.

SPRUCE IT UP

Satisfying snack: Baked sweet potato chips + egg-free aioli

Simple sandwich: Bread + sliced tomatoes + lettuce + cheddar cheese + egg-free aioli

Creamy dressing: Olive oil + apple cider vinegar + egg-free aioli

This dressing is tangy, creamy and sweet, livening up almost any veggie dish. And not simply as a condiment – toss with pumpkin, potato, cauliflower, carrots, etc. before roasting instead of using plain oil. I love that it doesn't contain eggs or dairy, like so many creamy dressings, meaning you can make a huge batch in mere minutes and keep calling on it for months to come (not that it seems to last that long!).

ZINGY MUSTARD DRESSING

1 garlic clove, peeled
100g apple cider vinegar
75g maple syrup
50g wholegrain mustard
50g Dijon mustard
2 teaspoons ground cumin
1 teaspoon ground turmeric
1 teaspoon ground coriander
1 teaspoon fine salt
½ teaspoon cayenne pepper
    (optional)
300g olive oil

MAKES 700ML

DAIRY FREE
GLUTEN FREE
VEGETARIAN
VEGAN

QUICK FIX

1.   Place garlic in TC bowl, chop for 4 seconds, speed 5.
2.   Add vinegar, maple syrup, mustards, spices and salt. Mix for 1 minute, speed 4, while slowly adding oil through the hole in the lid.

STORAGE

Transfer to a large bottle and store in the fridge for up to 6 months.

SPRUCE IT UP

Lunchbox: Soba noodles + grilled tofu + snow peas + shredded carrot + mustard dressing

Simple side salad: Salad greens + cucumber + avocado + mustard dressing

Bowl food: Diced roast pumpkin + green lentils + rocket + pumpkin seeds + mustard dressing

A little sweet, a little salty, a little tangy and very moreish! The cheat's version of satay sauce. Ellen has been known to load so much onto her dumplings that I'm not sure if the sauce or the dumpling is the accompaniment!

PEANUT DIPPING SAUCE

3cm piece ginger, peeled
140g unsweetened peanut
    butter
80g tamari or soy sauce
40g rice vinegar
40g maple syrup

MAKES 1 CUP

DAIRY FREE
GLUTEN FREE (OPTION)
VEGETARIAN
VEGAN

QUICK FIX

1. Place ginger in TC bowl, chop for 4 seconds, speed 6.
2. Add peanut butter, tamari or soy sauce, rice vinegar and maple syrup, mix for 10 seconds, speed 6.

TO SERVE

Store in the fridge for up to 1 month. The perfect accompaniment to gyoza (page 159), rice paper rolls, spring rolls, noodles, grilled meats and more.

NOTE

I prefer smooth peanut butter for this recipe, but crunchy also works.

SPRUCE IT UP

Rice paper rolls: Rice paper rounds + peanut dipping sauce + shredded cabbage + cucumber + mint

Satay noodles: Noodles + peanut dipping sauce + snow peas + spring onions + coriander

Tasty veggies: Steamed broccoli + peanut dipping sauce + sesame seeds

Thick, creamy and delicious yet this isn't really a mayo at all! It's missing the requisite egg yolk, instead relying on the tahini (ground sesame seeds) to thicken. In fact, it's creamier than most mayo and uses about a fifth of the oil.

SESAME MAYO

2 garlic cloves, peeled
200g hulled tahini
100g water
80g lemon juice (1–2 lemons)
60g olive oil
½ teaspoon fine salt

MAKES 1½ CUPS

DAIRY FREE
GLUTEN FREE
VEGETARIAN
VEGAN

QUICK FIX

1. Place garlic in TC bowl, chop for 3 seconds, speed 6.
2. Insert butterfly. Add tahini, water, lemon juice, oil and salt, mix for 1 minute, speed 4.

TO SERVE

Serve as a dressing, spread or dipping sauce alongside Asian and Middle Eastern dishes. Store in the fridge for up to 1 month.

SPRUCE IT UP

Falafel wrap: Pita bread + falafels (see page 15) + lettuce + tomato + sesame mayo

Moroccan salad: Roasted carrots + rocket + pomegranate arils + mint + sesame mayo

Sesame noodles: Soba noodles + grated carrot + red cabbage + edamame + sesame mayo

fermenting

Fermented foods and drinks are a staple in my
kitchen, both for the health benefits and the zingy taste!
Fermenting works by promoting the growth of good
bacteria, as opposed to pickling, which is focused
on inhibiting the growth of bad bacteria. By fermenting
foods not only can we hugely increase their shelf life,
but also their nutritional value and probiotic content.
Commercial products often don't offer nearly the
same benefit (or flavour!) that you get if you make
them yourself, not to mention they will cost you up
to ten times more. I know at first it's a strange concept,
but I've got some easy recipes to get you started.

I am such a huge fan of kombucha – I've been brewing it for the last six years, and never for a day have I not had a batch on the go. Once you get your SCOBY it really is one of the easiest ferments to do at home (big tick from me!) and it's also an easy one to incorporate into your daily routine – I love a glass as my 3 pm pickup. It also costs next to nothing to make yourself at home, which usually shocks people after they've seen the prices for store bought!

KOMBUCHA

160g raw organic sugar

1.7 litres filtered water

4 organic green or black tea
    bags

200g starter liquid (previously
    brewed kombucha, see note)

1 SCOBY (see note)

MAKES 1.8 LITRES

DAIRY FREE
GLUTEN FREE
VEGETARIAN
VEGAN

1. Place sugar and water in TC bowl, heat for 12 minutes, 80°C, speed 2 (100°C for black tea). Add tea bags and set aside to cool to room temperature (best left overnight).

2. Remove and discard tea bags. Pour cooled tea into a large glass jar or jug, of at least 2 litre capacity. Add starter liquid and SCOBY. Cover with a tea towel and secure with a rubber band.

3. Allow to sit undisturbed for 7–14 days out of direct sunlight. A second SCOBY will begin forming on the top of the liquid. Using a non-metal spoon, taste tea regularly until desired balance is reached between sweet and vinegary. The brew starts very sweet and slowly turns more tart. The warmer the temperature, the faster this will happen.

4. When ready, using clean hands, remove SCOBYs (you will now have 2) and transfer to a bowl along with 200ml of the fermented tea (this is your starter liquid for the next batch).

TO SERVE

Bottle remaining fermented tea — it is now ready for consumption — and store in refrigerator until ready to serve or do a second ferment. Put your next batch on!

NOTE

A SCOBY is a Symbiotic Colony of Yeast and Bacteria. You can buy one online or, better yet, find a friend who brews kombucha – they'll be more than happy to gift you one! Whenever you buy or are gifted a SCOBY it will always come submerged in kombucha – this is your starter liquid for your first batch.

Served on our
'dirty burger'
page 157.

Here I've given sauerkraut a flavour makeover, making it punchy and smoky – a whole new take on this classic. Perfect for adding big flavour and gut-loving benefits to a wide range of dishes. Of course, you could leave the apple and liquid smoke out and be left with a traditional sauerkraut recipe – I like having both on hand.

SMOKY APPLE SAUERKRAUT

1 green apple, quartered and cored
½ small white cabbage, thinly sliced (or ¼ large cabbage)
1½ tablespoons fine sea salt
1 teaspoon liquid smoke

MAKES 5 CUPS

DAIRY FREE
GLUTEN FREE
VEGETARIAN
VEGAN

NOTE

It is essential that the vegetables are completely submerged under the liquid, otherwise mould may grow on the top. If mould does grow, discard all vegetables and start again. Next time, knead vegetables longer and add more salt. Bubbles, white foam and white scum may form on top of the liquid – this is completely normal. Lift off with a spoon once fermentation is finished.

1. Place apple in TC bowl, grate for 5 seconds, speed 4.
2. Add as much cabbage as will fit in TC bowl, then add salt and smoke, knead for 1 minute, dough function.
3. Top up with as much cabbage as will fit, knead for 1 minute, dough function.
4. Top up with remaining cabbage, knead for 1 minute, dough function.
5. Squish the entire mixture (including all liquid) into a pickle press. Place the lid on and tighten the press down until the vegetables are firmly compacted and the liquids rise above the press, completely submerging the vegetables. If there isn't enough liquid, wait 30 minutes and tighten again. If you don't have a pickle press, use a fermentation crock or a large glass jar with a weight inside to push the vegetables down and hold in the liquid. Special dunking weights can be purchased, or use a small cup, bowl or plate.
6. Allow to sit out of direct sunlight, undisturbed, for 2–14 days. Taste every few days until fermented to your liking. The longer it sits, the less salty it will be and the stronger the pickled flavour.

TO SERVE

Transfer vegetables to an airtight jar, seal, and refrigerate until ready to serve. Fermented vegetables can be kept for up to a year in the fridge and improve with age. Serve on burgers, sandwiches and tacos, toss through coleslaws and salads, or garnish scrambled eggs and carbonara pasta.

I love making yoghurt from scratch. It's so economical that there's really no reason not to go for the organic milk. I promise it is super easy once you've given it a go – you'll be making it without the recipe soon! While I love the simplicity of my classic yoghurt recipe in *Quick Fix in the Thermomix* (the book that started it all!), the addition of kuzu in this version gives a luxurious smoothness and thickens it up without the need to drain.

SUPER-THICK YOGHURT

40g kuzu (see note)
1.8 litres full-fat organic milk
80g natural yoghurt (good
　　quality store brought or
　　homemade)
2.2 litres food warmer

MAKES 2 LITRES

GLUTEN FREE
VEGETARIAN

1.　Place kuzu in TC bowl, mill for 10 seconds, speed 10. Scrape down sides and lid.

2.　Add milk, cook for 60 minutes, 90°C, speed 2.5.

3.　Allow milk to cool by removing TC bowl from base and standing for at least 1 hour.

4.　Place TC bowl back on base and ensure no temperature is registering – milk must be below 37°C. Once cool, add yoghurt, mix for 5 seconds, speed 4.

5.　Cook for 12 minutes, 37°C, speed soft.

6.　Meanwhile, pre-warm food warmer with hot water.

7.　Immediately place yoghurt mixture in food warmer and leave at room temperature for 24 hours.

TO SERVE

Refrigerate for a minimum 12 hours before serving, either in the food warmer or decanted into jars. For a traditional 'pot set' yoghurt, keep it in the food warmer.

NOTE

Kuzu root, available from health food stores, is a cooking starch that beautifully thickens soups, stews, sauces and desserts, and in this case, yoghurt.

Fizzing, fresh
and healthy!

Bubbly, sweet and sour, this is just like your classic homemade lemonade, only much, much better for you! It really is magical how the good bacteria in the whey eat the sugar and produce carbon dioxide as a by-product, creating the most beautiful natural carbonation (with much less sugar in the final drink). The hiss and fizz when I first open a bottle never ceases to amaze me! There are so many great fermented drink options, but the reason I love this one so much is it's accessible to all – no need buy any special starter cultures, just make a batch of yoghurt. Give it a go – I really think you'll be impressed.

PROBIOTIC LEMONADE

100g raw sugar
4 lemons, juice only
1 litre water
100g whey (see note)

MAKES 1½ LITRES

GLUTEN FREE
VEGETARIAN

1. Place all ingredients in TC bowl, heat for 4 minutes, 37°C, speed 2.
2. Divide between flip-top bottles, seal tightly and leave in a warm place for 5–7 days to ferment.

TO SERVE

Once fermentation has finished, refrigerate bottles until ready to serve. Once bottles are opened they will lose some of their carbonation, so try not to even have a peek until you're ready to pour yourself a big glass and enjoy.

NOTE

Whey is the yellowish liquid left over after you strain yoghurt or cheese. To make your own, make a batch of homemade yoghurt (see page 59), then once set transfer to sieve or TC steamer basket lined with cheesecloth or paper towel. Allow to drain for 1–24 hours or until you've got the desired amount of whey and/or your yoghurt has thickened to the desired consistency. Leave it long enough, and you'll have yoghurt cheese! Make sure to sit your strainer inside a large bowl to catch the dripping whey.

The real name for this traditional Japanese seasoning is 'shio koji', but I figured fermented flavour bomb paste was a better descriptor for this book! It seems a little strange, but it's actually an incredibly easy ferment and one which is easily incorporated into your daily cooking, bringing out umami flavours in any dish. It is a probiotic, so excellent for gut health, and breaks down proteins and starches, tenderising and bringing out sweetness. For the most cucumber-y cucumber you've ever tasted, toss in flavour bomb paste, allow to sit for 15 minutes, then enjoy. A cucumber has never tasted so good!

FERMENTED FLAVOUR BOMB PASTE

150g dried rice koji (see note)
220g water
40g fine salt

MAKES 1 CUP

DAIRY FREE
GLUTEN FREE
VEGETARIAN
VEGAN

1. Place koji in TC bowl, mill for 2 minutes, speed 9.

2. Add water and salt, mix for 30 seconds, speed 4.

3. Transfer to a glass jar, cover with a piece of cloth and secure with a rubber band. Store in a warm spot for 7–10 days. Stir mixture once daily. Once it smells faintly like sweet soy sauce, cover with a tight lid and refrigerate for up to 6 months. The flavour will develop over time in the fridge and become milder and sweeter.

TO SERVE

To use, substitute 2 teaspoons of flavour bomb paste for 1 teaspoon of salt in recipes, or in a marinade to tenderise meat and fish. To lightly pickle vegetables, toss slices of cucumber, carrot, cabbage and radish in a little flavour bomb paste and wait 15 minutes before serving.

NOTE

Dried rice koji looks just like a bag of regular rice but is actually dried, fermented cooked rice. It is available from selected organic shops, health food stores, Japanese grocers and online stores.

If you don't have fine salt, simply add 40g coarse salt in at step 1 and mill with rice.

TURNING WASTE INTO FOOD

When you're cooking fresh using the recipes in this book, you'll find that the majority of your kitchen waste is compostable and full of nutrients – definitely not rubbish! This waste that would otherwise be destined for landfill can be broken down and used as a rich fertiliser to grow nutrient-dense food, all in your home garden. Think about the celery tops, the potato peels and the egg shells you put in the bin – these all contain precious vitamins and minerals! What a terrible shame for these valuable nutrients to rot in landfill and not be utilised.

I am evangelical about composting, even collecting compostable scraps at friends' dinner parties to take home! It just makes such sense to me – how can your food contain nutrients if the earth it is grown in doesn't? We can't keep taking from the soil without giving anything back. The power is in our hands as backyard gardeners to change things for the better, and for me it all starts with composting. In case you needed further convincing, carbon from the atmosphere (think global warming) can actually be sequestered into the earth and stored in organic matter (think compost!), reducing CO_2 levels. Composted soils also hold a significantly higher water content, meaning you can grow more food using less water!

To my mind, composting is another one of my ferments that I need to nurture – bacteria and other living organisms performing transformations, with the whole being much greater than the sum of the parts. I promise it is easy and, once set up, takes next to no time. Like all my ferments, it has become second nature. These are the two methods I use, the second working even if you are seriously limited with space!

Compost bins

If you've got outdoor space, a compost bin is the way to go. You can build your own wooden box or simply purchase a plastic compost drum. No matter what type of bin you choose, I always recommend having (at least) two, so you can leave one to break down and do its thing while you start filling up the next one – it will save a lot of effort in the long run. In a couple of months all that 'waste' will have turned into rich composted soil, ready to be added to your garden beds or pot plants.

Household waste such as fruit and vegetable scraps, tea bags, coffee grounds, eggshells, egg cartons, paper bags, cardboard boxes, newspapers, scrap paper, toilet roll inserts, tissues, paper towel, cut flowers and paper coffee cups can all be composted in the compost bin and saved from landfill. Imagine how much you could cut down your rubbish? You can also add garden waste, including autumn leaves, grass clippings and prunings, as well as straw/bedding from animal enclosures (rabbits, Guinea pigs and chickens).

Your compost should have a good mix of green and brown material – green being 'wet' material such as food scraps, and brown being 'dry' material such as paper. This will keep your compost moist. Too dry? Water it or add some more green material. Too wet? Find some old newspapers and shred them up before adding to your bin!

Worm farms

Even if you live in an apartment or small space and can't grow food, you can still turn your scraps into nutrient-dense fertiliser for your indoor plants by setting up a worm

How can your food
contain nutrients
if the soil it is
grown in doesn't?

farm on your balcony or in your garage (see page 123 for why you should have indoor plants and my favourites!). This is just as easy as composting, although you'll need to buy a box of live compost worms to get you started. I'd also recommend buying a purpose-built worm farm, especially if fitting it in a small space – there are plenty of different shapes and sizes available.

With a worm farm you feed the worms your scraps, and they excrete worm castings, which are gold for your plants. Just like other ferments, one's trash is another's treasure! Worm farms have a tap on the bottom that drains out excess liquid, so keep a bucket underneath to collect this 'worm tea'. Use this to water your plants and watch them grow! Remember to water your worms weekly, especially in hot weather, as they'll die if they dry out, and always leave the tap open as you don't want to drown them either. Like a compost bin, you want to keep it moist.

Don't forget to feed your worms – on average once a week, or whenever the last lot of food scraps have disappeared. Don't add so much food that it starts rotting before the worms have a chance to eat it all. They are a little fussier than your standard compost bin, not liking citrus or onion, and prefer their food in small bits. Rough-chop your scraps or, even better, chuck them all in your thermo cooker and blitz for 10 seconds, speed 9. Your worms will love you for it!

In the compost:
- Fruit scraps
- Vegetable scraps
- Tea bags
- Coffee grounds
- Juicing pulp
- Eggshells
- Egg cartons
- Cut flowers
- Paper coffee cups
- Biodegradable produce bags
- Paper
- Shredded newspaper
- Cardboard
- Toilet roll inserts
- Paper towel
- Tissues
- Straw
- Woodchips
- Leaves
- Grass clippings
- Plants
- Potting mix
- Wood ash
- Chicken poo
- Horse poo

In the worm farm:
- Fruit (not citrus)
- Vegetables (not onion)
- Shredded paper
- Shredded cardboard
- Crushed eggshells
- Coffee grounds
- Tea leaves
- Juicing pulp
- Bread
- Tissues
- Toilet roll inserts
- Leaves

Blitz up in the TC bowl, speed 9 for 10 seconds.

Composting is quite literally magic — you can grow food from waste!

SUMMER

Long days and balmy nights means more time outdoors and socialising under the sun. Snacks doubling as casual finger food and picnic fare are essential. Drinks become a staple – refreshing and sustaining in the heat. I also find myself creating plenty of fresh desserts in the warmer weather; there's no better time to make sweet treats to celebrate the abundance of fresh, juicy produce available.

My favourite summer produce:

Apricot	Lychee
Berries	Mango
Cantaloupe	Nectarine
Capsicum	Parsley
Cherries	Peach
Chilli	Passionfruit
Corn	Pineapple
Eggplant	Watermelon
Grapes	

in-betweens

Having delicious and nutritious homemade snacks on hand is so important to me, because when life gets busy it's all too easy to reach for something processed, packaged and filled with unwanted ingredients. That's why all the recipes in this chapter can be made in advance when you've got a little more time on your hands, then simply grabbed when you're busy and a little pick-me-up is needed. Many can be thrown in lunchboxes for snacks on the go, while others make perfect finger food when entertaining — same easy recipes, so many uses!

Everyone knows our office has a penchant for coconut chews – they are just such a moreish, nourishing and convenient snack! We've got variations in three of our cookbooks, but I reckon this is the most versatile option – being egg free and nut free makes it perfect for school lunches, vegans and anyone with allergies. I often have all the ingredients in the pantry meaning I can whip up a batch at a minute's notice, making it a very handy recipe to have up your sleeve.

COCONUT SEED CHEWS

20g sesame seeds
20g chia seeds
30g sunflower seeds
70g pumpkin seeds
180g shredded coconut
70g coconut sugar
55g coconut oil
20g rice malt syrup
1 teaspoon vanilla extract
¼ teaspoon fine salt
20g water

MAKES 24

DAIRY FREE
GLUTEN FREE
VEGETARIAN
VEGAN

QUICK FIX + COOLING

1. Preheat oven to 150°C. Line a baking tray with baking paper.
2. Place sesame seeds, chia seeds, sunflower seeds, 30g pumpkin seeds and 100g shredded coconut in TC bowl, mill for 8 seconds, speed 9.
3. Add coconut sugar, coconut oil, rice malt syrup, vanilla extract and salt, mix for 8 seconds, speed 7.
4. Add water, remaining 80g shredded coconut and remaining 40g pumpkin seeds. Mix for 6 seconds, reverse speed 3. Scrape down sides.
5. Mix for a further 6 seconds, reverse speed 3.
6. Place in small mounds on lined tray, leaving a 5 cm space between each. Use your hands or a spoon to help shape them.
7. Bake for 15 minutes, or until golden. Allow to cool completely on baking tray – they will firm up as they cool.

TO SERVE
Store in an airtight container for up to 1 week.

This would be one of my favourite bliss ball recipes – caramel-y without being overly sweet, and with just the right texture and little crunch. It's my sister Ellen's creation, and I love how she's made something nourishing and healthy taste anything but. I might also love them because things always taste better when someone else makes them for you!

SALTED CARAMEL BLISS BALLS

100g raw almonds
1 vanilla bean, halved
100g unsalted raw cashews
80g medjool dates, pitted (approx. 7)
30g desiccated coconut
40g buckwheat groats
35g maple syrup
10g water
1½ teaspoons salt flakes

MAKES ABOUT 25

DAIRY FREE
GLUTEN FREE
VEGETARIAN
VEGAN

QUICK FIX

1. Place almonds and vanilla bean in TC bowl, blitz for 10 seconds, speed 8.
2. Add cashews, dates, coconut, buckwheat groats, maple syrup, water and salt. Chop for 6 seconds, speed 8.
3. If mixture is looking too dry to stick together, add an extra teaspoon of water and mix for 2 seconds, speed 8.
4. Roll into snack-size balls using wet hands if mixture is sticking.

TO SERVE

Store in an airtight container in the fridge for 1 week, or freeze for up to 6 months.

VARIATION

For a chocolaty variation, roll finished balls in cacao or cocoa (pictured).

NOTE

Buckwheat groats, sometimes known as buckinis, can be found in health food stores.

Remember those sesame snaps from childhood? Well this is my revamped, more nutritious version! It's a delicious combination of healthy nuts and seeds, bound together with sweet honey or maple syrup. I love one of these as a satisfying afternoon snack, and I think you and your family will too!

SEED BARK

150g raw almonds
100g pumpkin seeds
100g sunflower seeds
100g chia seeds
75g sesame seeds
50g flaxseeds
25g poppy seeds
150g honey or maple syrup
30g macadamia oil
¼ teaspoon fine salt

MAKES 20 PIECES

DAIRY FREE
GLUTEN FREE
VEGETARIAN
VEGAN

QUICK FIX + COOLING

1. Preheat oven to 140°C.

2. Place almonds in TC bowl, chop 2 seconds, speed 7.

3. Add remaining ingredients to TC bowl, mix for 20 seconds, reverse speed 3. Pack mixture firmly onto a large baking tray lined with baking paper or a baking mat. Use wet hands or a wet silicone spatula to tightly pack into a single sheet.

4. Bake for 15 minutes, then turn off oven. Allow mixture to cool completely inside the oven – do not open oven during this time.

TO SERVE

Once cooled, break or cut seed bark into snack-sized pieces. Transfer to a glass jar or container for storage.

*Same recipe, so many
different flavours.*

Gelatine is all the rage for gut health, and here's how I include it in my diet – fruit jellies! These are a really satisfying sweet treat and surprisingly are filled with protein and collagen. I've written this as a guide rather than a recipe because whatever your family's favourite fruit flavours are, do that! Or whatever you've got on hand – this is a great way to use up little bits and pieces in the fridge. Look for grass-fed beef gelatine from the health food store, not from the baking aisle of the supermarket.

FRUIT JELLIES

6 tablespoons powdered gelatine

300g fruit juice (not kiwi or pineapple)

150g fresh or frozen fruit – raspberries, blueberries, peaches, apricots, watermelon, mango, banana or pear

200g extra liquid – fruit juice, coconut water, coconut milk, thin yoghurt or thin cream

20g sweetener – raw sugar, white sugar, coconut sugar, xylitol, honey, maple syrup, agave syrup or coconut nectar

MAKES 60

DAIRY FREE (OPTION)
GLUTEN FREE

QUICK FIX + COOLING

1. Combine gelatine and 300g fruit juice in a small bowl. Set aside.
2. Place fruit, extra liquid and sweetener in TC bowl, purée for 5 seconds, speed 7.
3. Heat for 4 minutes, 70°C, speed 3, or until 70°C reached.
4. Add gelatine and fruit juice mixture, mix for 20 seconds, speed 3. Pour into chocolate moulds or a large shallow plastic container and refrigerate for 2 hours or until set.

TO SERVE

Turn out fruit jellies by peeling the edges away from the moulds. If you've used a large container you'll need to cut the gummies into snack-sized squares. Store in the fridge for up to 1 week.

NOTE

Depending on the sweetness of the fruit and extra liquid used, you may need to add extra sweetener. You can taste for sweetness at step 3 and add more if needed.

I love the simplicity of this recipe, highlighting the fresh produce – in this case tomatoes and zucchini. The tarts are so easy to whip up, especially handy for social get-togethers as they can be enjoyed with fingers, no cutlery required!

SIMPLE SUMMER TARTS

2 sheets butter puff pastry

100g cheese, roughly chopped – parmesan, cheddar, tasty, feta

Small handful fresh herbs, leaves only – thyme, rosemary, basil, parsley

120g mascarpone cheese

1 teaspoon fine salt, plus extra, to taste

300g vegetables, thinly sliced – zucchini, tomatoes, asparagus, red onion, capsicum, mushrooms, broccoli

30g olive oil

MAKES 8

VEGETARIAN

QUICK FIX

1. Preheat oven to 200°C. Line 2 oven trays with baking paper or baking mats.

2. Cut each pastry sheet into 4 squares and place on trays. Lightly score a 1cm border around each square.

3. Place cheese and herbs (not basil or parsley) in TC bowl, grate for 5 seconds, speed 8.

4. Add mascarpone and salt, mix for 5 seconds, speed 4.

5. Using the back of a spoon, spread the cheese mixture across the centre of each pastry square, keeping the 1cm border clear. Toss vegetables in olive oil and extra salt, then layer on top.

6. Bake for 15 minutes, or until pastry is puffed and golden.

TO SERVE

Garnish with basil or parsley (if using). Delicious served straight away but can also be made up to 3 days in advance and stored in an airtight container in the fridge. Serve cold or reheat in a moderate oven.

NOTE

This recipe easily scales up – follow exactly the same instructions with more ingredients.

With a little fire and a whole lot of flavour, this dip is a crowd favourite! The roasted eggplant gives it a creamy base, while the harissa paste adds North African heat and spice. You can make your own harissa – it's a blend of roasted red capsicum and aromatics – or you can buy a jar from the delicatessen. My recipe is in one of my earlier cookbooks, *Quick Fix: Every Occasion*.

HARISSA EGGPLANT DIP

1 large eggplant, roughly
    chopped into 2cm pieces
30g macadamia oil
1 teaspoon fine salt
3 garlic cloves, unpeeled
60g walnuts
80g harissa paste
1 lemon, juice only
30g olive oil
10g coconut sugar

MAKES 1½ CUPS

DAIRY FREE
GLUTEN FREE
VEGETARIAN
VEGAN

QUICK FIX + ROASTING

1. Preheat oven to 190°C.
2. Place eggplant in large roasting tray and toss with macadamia oil and salt. Roast for 25 minutes.
3. Add garlic and walnuts to oven tray and roast with eggplant for a further 5 minutes.
4. Squeeze garlic from skins into TC bowl. Add eggplant, walnuts, harissa paste, lemon juice, olive oil and coconut sugar. Blend for 10 seconds, speed 6.

TO SERVE
Serve immediately for a warm dip, or refrigerate and serve cold. Garnish with toasted pine nuts, sesame seeds or an extra drizzle of olive oil.

NOTE
This recipe easily scales up – follow exactly the same instructions with more ingredients.

These little cuties are such an easy snack on the go, already portioned out for you! I've used macadamia oil and spelt flour to keep them wheat and dairy free and, like with most of the recipes in this book, I'm relying on the natural flavour and sweetness to come primarily from the fresh produce. Best enjoyed warm out of the oven with lashings of organic butter.

MINI SPELT BANANA BREADS

1 vanilla bean, halved
½ cinnamon stick
75g brown sugar
4 bananas, ripened until black
2 free-range eggs
120g macadamia oil
250g wholemeal spelt flour
2 teaspoons baking powder
¼ teaspoon fine salt

MAKES 12

DAIRY FREE
VEGETARIAN

1. Preheat oven to 175°C.
2. Place vanilla bean, cinnamon and sugar in TC bowl, mill for 30 seconds, speed 10.
3. Add bananas, eggs and oil, mix for 5 seconds, speed 5.
4. Add flour, baking powder and salt, mix for 10 seconds, speed 4. Scrape down sides.
5. Mix for a further 10 seconds, speed 3. Divide mixture evenly between 12 silicone bar moulds, bake for 25 minutes, or until a skewer inserted comes out clean.
6. Allow breads to sit in moulds for a minimum of 10 minutes before turning out and allowing to cool on a wire rack.

TO SERVE

Enjoy fresh or gently warmed in a moderate oven for 10 minutes. Delicious as it is, but even better with butter!

NOTE

Most of the flavour and sweetness in this recipe is coming from the bananas, so it's essential that they're ripened to black. Perfect for bananas too ripe to eat fresh!

VARIATION

For one large loaf, pour mixture into a baking paper-lined loaf tin and bake for 50 minutes, or until a skewer inserted comes out clean.

Some of my favourite summer days.

sweet somethings

With simple combinations of ingredients, these sweet recipes let the summer fruit shine. Here I've focused on fresh produce to bring all the flavour – think fresh sorbets and fruity tarts. As always, I've got quick recipes to whip up on the spot, plus many lavish options to make in advance, ready for entertaining or when a sweet treat is in order. Remember, homemade is always best, and everyone's got room for dessert!

People regularly ask where my inspiration for recipes come from, and often it's a badgering family member! My sister Loryn wanted a healthy lemon tart recipe, so this was Ellen's creation. I was so impressed that I cut it from the draft of her vegan e-book and included it here. It is satisfying and delicious, yet actually nutritious! There might be a few 'what the heck is that' ingredients but I promise you, buy them from the health food store, stock them in your pantry and, aside from the lemons, you'll have everything you need to make this tart time and time again.

LORYN'S LEMON TART

100g raw almonds
100g quinoa flakes
100g desiccated coconut
50g raw macadamia nuts
10 medjool dates, pitted
40g solid coconut oil
2 lemons, rind only
1 vanilla bean, halved
¼ teaspoon fine salt
20g kuzu
15g cornflour
2 teaspoons agar powder
200g coconut cream
125g lemon juice (approx.
    3 large lemons)
140g maple syrup
60g rice malt syrup

SERVES 8

DAIRY FREE
GLUTEN FREE
VEGETARIAN
VEGAN

1. Place almonds, quinoa flakes, coconut, macadamia nuts, dates, coconut oil, rind of 1 lemon, vanilla bean and salt in TC bowl. Chop for 30 seconds, speed 8, or until it forms a moist crumb-like texture.

2. Press crust mixture firmly down into base and sides of a 24 cm loose-bottom tart tin. Refrigerate while you make the filling.

3. Place remaining lemon rind, kuzu and cornflour in a clean TC bowl. Mill for 40 seconds, speed 10. Scrape down sides and lid.

4. Add agar powder, coconut cream, lemon juice, maple syrup and rice malt syrup. Cook for 10 minutes, 90°C, speed 4.

5. Pour filling on top of tart crust and refrigerate for a minimum 3 hours, or until filling has set.

TO SERVE

Dust with icing sugar just prior to serving. Can be served straight from the fridge although not necessary – once the tart has set it will hold its shape at room temperature. Store in an airtight container in the fridge for 5 days.

I could have included one delicious ice-cream recipe here, but why stop at just one when there are so many amazing flavours! With my recipe as the framework, let your imagination run wild and experiment with the bounty of summer fruits available. To extend this recipe beyond summer, roughly chop and freeze fruit when it's at its seasonal peak and tastiest – that's usually also when it's cheapest, so it's an easy one. Head to your local farmers market and a quick glance of what's plentiful will tell you what's at its prime.

EASY ICE-CREAM

50g sweetener of your choice
 – white sugar, raw sugar, coconut sugar, maple syrup, xylitol, honey, rice malt syrup
2 bananas, halved and frozen
300g frozen fruit, roughly chopped – mango, peaches, nectarines, apricots, plums, raspberries, blueberries, strawberries, pineapple, extra banana
100g creamy component – yoghurt, coconut cream, coconut yoghurt, cream, milk, soy milk

SERVES 4

DAIRY FREE (OPTION)
GLUTEN FREE
VEGETARIAN
VEGAN (OPTION)

QUICK FIX + FREEZING

1. Place sweetener in TC bowl, mill for 10 seconds, speed 9. If using liquid sweetener skip this step.

2. Add bananas, frozen fruit and creamy component, mix for 10 seconds, speed 9, assisting with spatula if necessary.

3. Continue mixing for 1 minute, speed 6, or until mixture comes together and looks like ice-cream.

TO SERVE

Serve immediately, or return to the freezer for up to 2 hours for firmer scoops.

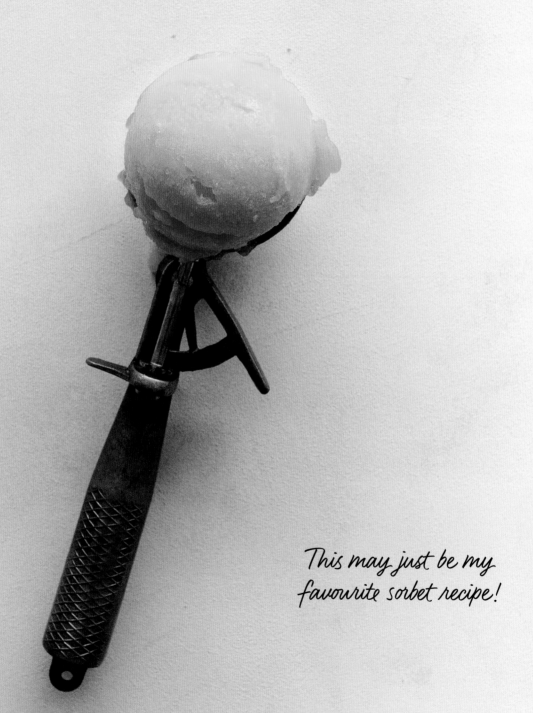

This may just be my
favourite sorbet recipe!

Just like you get in the punnet from the supermarket! I absolutely adore homemade sorbets done in the thermo cooker, but the problem is you always have to emulsify or re-emulsify right before serving, which is sometimes a pain. This recipe stays smooth and scoopable straight out of the freezer for months, meaning you can scoop out a delicious spoonful whenever you like. I've been experimenting with this formula for years to get the perfect texture, and finally I've got it just right.

SCOOPABLE MANGO SORBET

100g raw sugar
1kg mango flesh, roughly
    chopped and frozen (see
    note)
30g rum, vodka or gin
150g glucose syrup

SERVES 8

DAIRY FREE
GLUTEN FREE
VEGETARIAN
VEGAN

QUICK FIX + FREEZING

1. Place sugar in TC bowl, mill for 10 seconds, speed 10.
2. Add half the frozen mango, alcohol and glucose syrup, purée for 30 seconds, speed 9, assisting with spatula if necessary.
3. Add the remaining frozen mango, purée for 30 seconds, speed 9, assisting with spatula if necessary. Scrape down sides.
4. Purée for a further 30 seconds, speed 9, assisting with spatula if necessary, or until smooth. Transfer to a shallow container and freeze until ready to serve (minimum 4 hours).

TO SERVE

Remove from freezer and scoop straight out of the container. Perfect for ice-cream cones.

NOTE

It is essential that your mango is frozen before starting this recipe. You can either chop up fresh mangoes and freeze, or buy already frozen mango. If buying frozen, ensure they are Australian mangoes, as these taste the best!

*My favourite combination
is yellow peaches and
raspberry jam.*

Stunning in all its simplicity, this tart highlights the beautiful summer stone fruit with nothing more than fruit and a touch of jam in the filling. The pastry itself is a work of genius created by my mum, Janene, and has the perfect shortcrust texture while being dairy free, refined-sugar free and wheat free. This is dessert so healthy you really could eat it for breakfast!

FREE-FORM SUMMER FRUIT TART

100g raw almonds
90g maple syrup
90g coconut oil
125g wholemeal spelt flour
90g quinoa flour
¼ teaspoon baking powder
Pinch salt
2 teaspoons rosewater
5 tablespoons jam
5 ripe stone fruit, each cut into
    16 segments – apricots,
    peaches, nectarines, plums
Raw sugar, to garnish

SERVES 10

DAIRY FREE
VEGETARIAN
VEGAN

NOTE

As we are relying so heavily on the fruit to bring the flavour to this tart, ensure that your fruit is ripe, juicy and delicious.

1. Place almonds in TC bowl, mill for 5 seconds, speed 8. Remove from TC bowl and set aside.
2. Without cleaning TC bowl, add maple syrup and coconut oil, melt for 3 minutes, 50°C, speed 1.
3. Add spelt flour, quinoa flour, baking powder, salt, rosewater and reserved almond meal, mix for 7 seconds, speed 4.
4. Tip pastry onto a baking mat or a piece of cling film and squeeze together to shape into a disc. Wrap up and refrigerate for 30 minutes.
5. Preheat oven to 180°C, heating from the base of the oven if possible.
6. Unwrap chilled pastry and transfer to a 50cm-long piece of baking paper. Top with another piece of baking paper or cling film and roll out to form a circle approximately 30cm in diameter. Remove top cover and transfer to a baking tray. Spread jam evenly across the pastry using the back of a spoon, leaving a 5cm border around the outside. Top jam centre with fruit, then fold all edges in by folding the baking paper up to form sides. Be gentle with the pastry, but it will crack in parts which is fine. Sprinkle top with raw sugar.
7. Bake for 40 minutes, or until pastry is golden and fruit is cooked. If your tart is browning too quickly on the top (especially likely if not using bottom heat), cover loosely with foil.

TO SERVE

Allow to cool for a minimum 10 minutes before slicing into wedges and serving. Serve with cream, coconut yoghurt, ice-cream or fruit coulis. Also delicious served cold.

We love these
edible pansies!

Who needs artificial colours and flavours when you've got fresh, juicy pineapples in season? This recipe so embodies summer, refreshing and delighting kids and adults alike. I still get excited about how easy it is to powder ice in the thermo cooker.

PINA COLADA SNOW CONES

300g ripe pineapple, roughly chopped
120g raw sugar
100g coconut milk
1 lime, juice only
¼ teaspoon ground turmeric (optional, for colour only)
1kg ice cubes

MAKES 400ML SYRUP

DAIRY FREE
GLUTEN FREE
VEGETARIAN
VEGAN

QUICK FIX + CHILLING

1. Place pineapple and sugar in TC bowl, purée for 10 seconds, speed 9. Scrape down sides.

2. Cook for 10 minutes, steaming temperature, speed 1, MC removed and steamer basket on top to prevent splashes.

3. Add coconut milk, lime juice and turmeric (if using), mix for 10 seconds, speed 8. Strain through a fine sieve to remove pineapple pulp and refrigerate until completely chilled.

4. When ready to serve, place ice in TC bowl, mill for 10 seconds, speed 7, or until ice powder is formed.

TO SERVE

Divide ice between cups or paper cones and drizzle with pina colada syrup. Serve immediately.

VARIATION

Add a shot of coconut-flavoured rum to each adult snow cone for a summer cocktail.

NOTE

The pineapple brings all the flavour to this recipe – ensure it is sweet, ripe and juicy. If you're looking for a vibrant snow cone, add the turmeric – it gives a bright yellow colour and, don't worry, you can't taste it!

The real deal, made with real fresh, whole raspberries! I've even left the raspberry seeds in just to prove it. These are so beautifully coloured, scented and flavoured, even I was amazed by what a single punnet of raspberries could do! Marshmallows are such an impressive thing to make yourself, yet they are really quite easy with a thermo cooker, requiring only patience.

RASPBERRY MARSHMALLOWS

200g water
30g powdered gelatine
560g white sugar
125g fresh raspberries
60g white sugar
20g cornflour

MAKES 36

DAIRY FREE
GLUTEN FREE

1. Place 150g water and gelatine in a small bowl and stir. Set aside.
2. Place 500g sugar in TC bowl, mill for 10 seconds, speed 10.
3. Add remaining 50g water, raspberries and gelatine mixture, cook for 20 minutes, 100°C, speed 2, MC removed. Cool mixture in TC bowl until there is no registered temperature (below 37°C). This will take several hours.
4. Once cool, insert butterfly. Beat for 5 minutes, speed 4.
5. Line a square cake tin (approximately 25 x 25cm) with baking paper, leaving sides overhanging. Pour mixture into lined tin. Refrigerate for a minimum of 4 hours, or until set.
6. Meanwhile, place remaining 60g sugar and cornflour in TC bowl, mill for 10 seconds, speed 9. Set aside in a large bowl ready to dust marshmallows.

TO SERVE

Cut into squares and toss in sugar mixture. Store in an airtight container in the fridge for up to 2 weeks.

NOTE

If marshmallow sticks to your knife while cutting, dust both the knife and marshmallow in sugar and cornflour mixture first. You may also want to dust your hands before handling!

My baby sister
Ellen!

I just cannot get enough of sweet treats on a stick – you can make them ages in advance, and there are no dishes to do after they're served! Here I've kept things super light and refreshing, blending whole fruit to keep all the fibre and goodness in (you won't find that at your milk bar!) There's nothing better on a hot afternoon.

PINE-LIME WATERMELON POPS

250g watermelon, roughly
    chopped
150g pineapple, roughly
    chopped
30g maple syrup
1 lime, ½ juiced, ½ thinly sliced

MAKES 6

DAIRY FREE
GLUTEN FREE
VEGETARIAN
VEGAN

QUICK FIX + FREEZING

1. Place watermelon, pineapple, maple syrup and lime juice in TC bowl, blend for 1 minute, speed 9.

2. Stir to dissolve foam, then divide mixture between 6 ice-cream moulds. Top with a slice of lime and freeze for a minimum 6 hours.

TO SERVE

Remove from moulds and serve immediately, or transfer to an airtight container and store in the freezer for up to 6 months.

NOTE

We use silicone ice-cream moulds for all our frozen goodies!

refreshing

My collection of drinks to nourish, refresh, energise
and celebrate, making the most of the beautiful
warm-weather produce. Some double as breakfast,
while others could be dessert. I love how fuss-free
they are to whip up, meaning you're never far from
something fresh, fruity and refreshing.

This milkshake tastes way more indulgent than it actually is thanks to the frozen bananas, which become super creamy once blended and offer natural sweetness. It's essential to use ripe bananas, even possibly overripe bananas, so it's a cause for celebration if you've let a couple go a little too long in the fruit bowl. This drink may be icy cold and refreshing, but it's also pretty substantial – you might find it doubles as a meal on the go.

PEANUT BUTTER BANANA THICKSHAKE

2 ripe bananas, halved and
    frozen
400g milk of your choice
    – cow's, soy, almond, rice
200g ice
80g natural peanut butter
40g honey or maple syrup, or
    to taste
2 teaspoons vanilla extract
½ teaspoon ground cinnamon
¼ teaspoon fine salt

SERVES 2

DAIRY FREE (OPTION)
GLUTEN FREE
VEGETARIAN
VEGAN (OPTION)

QUICK FIX

1. Place all ingredients in TC bowl, purée for 1 minute, speed 9.

TO SERVE
Pour into 2 tall glasses and sip through a wide straw. You can also pour into an insulated bottle and enjoy as a breakfast on the go.

VARIATION
Peanut butter can be replaced with any other nut butter of your choice.

While oranges are generally considered winter fruit, the Valencia orange grows in summer and is one of the best oranges for juicing, so I couldn't resist including fresh orange juice!

Whenever I feel sluggish and in need of a boost, this is my go-to concoction. It's perfect first thing in the morning, but makes an equally good drink throughout the day. Raw beetroot is incredibly detoxifying, especially for the liver, yet not something that's easy to include in the diet. But purée it up, add some sweet fruit flavours and you're set!

FEEL-GOOD JUICE

200g beetroot, peeled and
    roughly chopped
100g frozen raspberries
1 lemon, peeled and pips
    removed
500g fresh orange juice

SERVES 2

DAIRY FREE
GLUTEN FREE
VEGETARIAN
VEGAN

QUICK FIX

1. Place beetroot, raspberries, lemon and 100g orange juice in TC bowl, purée for 30 seconds, speed 9.
2. Continue puréeing for 1 minute, speed 9, while slowing pouring remaining juice through the hole in the TC lid.

TO SERVE

Enjoy immediately or transfer to an insulated flask to sip throughout the day (in which case give it a gentle shake before drinking).

VARIATION

This drink is quite tart thanks to the lemon, but you can always add a splash of maple syrup or honey to sweeten.

Sprinkle with chia seeds
for extra protein.

My sister Ellen initially developed this recipe for another project, but after Loryn took the photo we all fell so in love with it we just had to squeeze it in here! Both the recipe and the photo totally embody the freshness I imagined for this book. It makes a refreshing afternoon sweet treat, but also a delicious summer breakfast.

TROPICAL GREEN SMOOTHIE BOWL

200g mango flesh, roughly chopped and frozen (approx. 2 mangoes, see note)

100g coconut cream

2 medjool dates, pitted

50g baby spinach

½ lime, juice only

1 teaspoon spirulina or chlorella, or other green powder (optional)

SERVES 2

DAIRY FREE
GLUTEN FREE
VEGETARIAN
VEGAN

QUICK FIX

1. Place all ingredients in TC bowl and purée for 30 seconds, speed 8, assisting with spatula if necessary.
2. Scrape down sides and blend for a further 1 minute, speed 6.

TO SERVE

Divide among 2 small serving bowls and top with fresh fruit, nuts, seeds, coconut flakes, granola, yoghurt, extra coconut cream, or whatever you've got on hand!

NOTE

You can buy mango already frozen, but check the label to ensure it's Australian mango – the imported ones never taste anywhere near as good!

Cheers!

This cocktail is a warm-weather favourite – cold and icy with a fresh zing of lime and passionfruit. The thermo cooker makes powdering ice a piece of cake, meaning the whole thing is ready in next to no time. The frozen lime definitely gives a thick and icy texture, but in a pinch simply use fresh lime juice – it will still taste amazing, but might be a little more 'passionfruit margarita' and a little less 'frozen'. We all had a little too much fun testing this recipe on photoshoot days!

FROZEN PASSIONFRUIT MARGARITA

50g white sugar

600g ice cubes

2 limes, juice only, frozen into ice cubes

200g tequila (or to taste)

4 passionfruit, pulp only

1. Place sugar in TC bowl, mill for 10 seconds, speed 10.

2. Add ice cubes, frozen lime juice and tequila, blend for 30 seconds, speed 9. Divide half the mixture between 4 glasses.

3. Add passionfruit pulp to remaining mixture and fold through using spatula. Divide evenly on top of white mixture.

SERVES 4

DAIRY FREE
GLUTEN FREE
VEGETARIAN
VEGAN

QUICK FIX

TO SERVE

Enjoy immediately, or transfer mixture to a shallow container and freeze for up to 2 hours before serving.

Watermelon is synonymous with summer, and there is nothing more refreshing than this slushie! I'm not the only one who likes to cool down with a watermelon treat – my pet chickens also love pecking on a frozen piece of watermelon on a hot day.

WATERMELON CRUSH

25g raw sugar (optional)
500g watermelon, roughly
    chopped and frozen
250g juice – apple, cranberry,
    orange, pineapple
1 lime, juice only

SERVES 3

DAIRY FREE
GLUTEN FREE
VEGETARIAN
VEGAN

QUICK FIX

1. Place sugar in TC bowl, mill for 10 seconds, speed 10.
2. Add remaining ingredients, purée for 30 seconds, speed 9, assisting with spatula.

TO SERVE

Pour into tall glasses and enjoy through a wide (non-disposable) straw. Best served straight away to enjoy that frozen texture.

VARIATION

For an adult option, add 100g of white rum, vodka or gin at step 2 and decrease fruit juice to 150g.

To my mind, this is one of the easiest ways to enjoy fresh turmeric and ginger – you don't even need to peel them! This elixir is packed with a powerhouse of ingredients including spicy ginger, detoxifying apple cider vinegar, lemon juice and healing honey. Enjoy first thing in the morning in warm water or add to soda water for a sparkling treat.

TURMERIC ELIXIR

8cm knob ginger, washed
8cm knob turmeric, washed
200g apple cider vinegar
120g raw honey
1 lemon, juice only

MAKES 350ML

DAIRY FREE
GLUTEN FREE
VEGETARIAN
VEGAN (OPTION)

1. Place ginger and turmeric in TC bowl, grate for 3 seconds, speed 6. Scrape down sides.

2. Add vinegar, honey and lemon juice, heat for 10 minutes, 37°C, speed 1. Allow to stand for minimum 30 minutes before straining through a fine sieve. Refrigerate until ready to serve.

TO SERVE

To serve, mix 1 part turmeric elixir to 6 parts warm water or soda water (or to taste).

VARIATION

For a vegan option, replace honey with maple syrup.

NOTE

To increase the goodness in the turmeric, add ½ teaspoon black pepper at step 2.

Keeping cooking quick, easy and fuss-free is
essential to me, so I've still got time to enjoy
all of the wonderful things in life.

Ditching chemicals is not
only better for you, but
better for everyone (including
this little lady!).

A FRESH HOME

One of the many reasons I love cooking my own food is that I know exactly what's in it and where it's come from, and I take the same approach with my cleaning and personal care products. Where possible I make my own, relying on everyday household ingredients and 100% pure essential oils. My home is fresh as a daisy, without any harsh chemicals in sight!

- **Kitchen cleaning spray.** Combine 250g water, 250g white vinegar and 25 drops lemon or orange essential oil in a 500ml spray bottle. Shake before each use. Mist onto benchtop, stovetop, cupboards, sink, etc. and wipe clean using a microfibre cloth.

- **Bathroom cleaning spray.** Combine 250g water, 250g white vinegar and 25 drops tea tree essential oil in a 500ml spray bottle. Shake before each use. Mist onto mirror, shower, floor, bath, sink, etc. and wipe clean using a microfibre cloth.

- **Floor cleaning spray.** Combine 250g water, 250g white vinegar and 25 drops eucalyptus essential oil in a 500ml spray bottle. Shake before each use. Mist over floors and wipe clean using a microfibre mop.

- **Sleep spray.** Combine 100g rosewater (the same type you use to make Turkish delight!) and 15 drops lavender essential oil in a small spray bottle. Shake before each use. Mist over pillow before bed for a deep sleep.

- **Face toner.** Mix equal parts apple cider vinegar and water in a spray or dropper bottle. Use a cotton pad or reusable face cloth to apply to face after cleansing.

- **Face spray.** Mix equal parts orange blossom water (the type you get from the deli) and water in a spray bottle and mist face during the day to refresh. I even use it to set my make-up!

- **Body moisturiser.** Use olive oil or coconut oil as a body moisturiser. I like to add in a couple of drops of lavender essential oil. Be careful to let the oil absorb before getting dressed in any nice clothes!

Another simple way I keep things fresh is to open windows and air the house out. I try to do it every day, even if just for an hour. Surprisingly, indoor air is significantly more toxic than outdoor air. Fresh air also helps to keep mold at bay.

My final fresh approach is to keep lots of indoor plants – like trees, these purify the air, and reduce molds. My picks are peace lilies in humid areas such as the bathroom, boston ferns anywhere there is indirect sunlight and parlor palms in low light. Cacti and succulents are easy as they'll forgive you if you forget to water them. I've also had success growing aloe vera and chilli inside; just position them next to a sunny window. Self-watering pots are my favourite for indoors as they combine the pot and the saucer in one unit, ensuring that neither the plant's feet nor your floors get wet! They're not quite as 'set and forget' as the name sounds, but they do make things much easier.

AUTUMN

The ever-changing days of autumn, filled with their glorious golden leaves, would have to be my favourite time of year. The garden is at its absolute peak with more beautiful fresh produce than I can keep up with, and some of my favourites come into season for the only time all year. Make the most of all that produce and get preserving, savouring the goodness for enjoyment throughout the cooler months. Now's also the time to stock up the freezer with delicious and nutritious meals ready to defrost in a flash later.

My favourite autumn produce:

Fig

Kiwifruit

Mushroom

Pomegranate

Quince

Parsnip

Persimmon

Plum

Pumpkin

Raspberries

Rhubarb

Sweet potato

Squash

Tamarillo

Tomato

larder love

Preserving is the ultimate celebration of fresh produce, so of course it needed its own chapter in this book! You are taking produce at its absolute seasonal best and preserving it for use throughout the less bountiful months, particularly winter. This once-forgotten art has had a complete resurgence, and it's never been easier than with the help of your thermo cooker. If you grow your own produce, like I do, preserving is essential during the glut of the harvest. If not, head to your local market and look around – if there's plenty of tomatoes everywhere, they must be at their best. Now of course you can go to the supermarket and buy tomatoes 365 days of the year, but I promise they will never be as rich, vibrant and flavoursome as when they're in season. So grab produce at its peak and preserve that essence!

As always, my mum Janene has exceeded herself with this recipe, and after much extensive testing I can safely agree this is the best way to make thermo passata! However, the most important factor is not the recipe but the tomatoes themselves – they must be red, ripe and juicy; Romas are my pick. Look for big boxes going cheap at markets – these are usually at optimum ripeness for passata. Once you've tasted this freshly made sauce, I promise you'll never go back to the purchased bottles. It's so flavoursome that I love it as a pasta sauce all on its own!

TOMATO PASSATA

1.5kg very ripe red tomatoes, roughly chopped
1 teaspoon salt
1 teaspoon sugar

MAKES 1 LITRE

DAIRY FREE
GLUTEN FREE
VEGETARIAN
VEGAN

1. Place tomatoes, salt and sugar in TC bowl, cook for 1 hour, 100°C, speed soft, MC removed and steamer basket on top to prevent splashes.

2. Purée for 15 seconds, speed 9.

TO SERVE

Pour into sterilised bottles and store in the fridge, or freeze in ice cube trays so you can defrost the exact amount you need. Use in pasta sauces, stews, soups, curries, pizza bases, lasagne etc.

NOTE

I always keep the empty glass jars when I finish things like mustard, coconut oil and passata, and re-use them to bottle my homemade chutneys and other flavour makers. Give the jars a good clean out, removing all leftover food particles, then run through the dishwasher on the hottest cycle to sterilise. Alternatively, soak in boiling water for a few minutes.

VARIATION

Add fresh chillies, garlic cloves or basil leaves at step 1.

My plum paste!

A fruit paste rounds out a cheese platter so perfectly, adding a delicious morsel of fragrant sweetness. While quince paste is by far the most common, plum paste is equally delicious, and much easier to make! A perfect batch cook when plums are at their peak, it will cost you cents on the dollar to cook at home and you'll have a taste of summer to last throughout the cooler months. It doesn't matter what variety you use, just look for the ones that look best. I also love this recipe for edible gifting – wrap bars in baking paper and secure with twine or set paste in little pots or jars.

PLUM PASTE

1kg plums, cored and roughly
    chopped
50g water
1 lemon, juice only
650g sugar (approx.)

MAKES 12 BARS

DAIRY FREE
GLUTEN FREE
VEGETARIAN
VEGAN

1. Place plums, water and lemon juice in TC bowl, cook for 30 minutes, 100°C, speed 1.

2. Remove mixture from TC bowl. Activate the scales and weigh back in the pulp. Add ¾ of the weight of the fruit in sugar. Purée mixture for 30 seconds, speed 9.

3. Cook for 1 hour, steaming temperature, speed 3, MC removed and steamer basket on top to prevent splashes.

4. Pour into 12 silicone bar moulds or a shallow tray greased or lined with baking paper. Refrigerate for 2 hours or until set.

TO SERVE

Serve plum paste as part of a cheese platter. Also great for creating a jammy centre inside doughnuts, cupcakes and muffins. Wrap individual bars in baking paper and store in an airtight container in the refrigerator for up to 1 year.

We've added slices of pink grapefruit, raspberries, mint and gin to our cooler, making it the ultimate warm weather cocktail.

This cordial is a sophisticated take on the classic lemonade – sweet and sour all at once, but also with fragrant, bitter and spicy hints from the rhubarb, ginger and orange. The resulting natural pretty pink hue was a surprise even to me! Rhubarb may not be the most versatile of plants, but it is one of the only vegetables that you plant once and it will keep delivering goodness year after year, making it one of my favourites.

RHUBARB CORDIAL

1 lemon, rind and juice
2 oranges, rind and juice
4cm piece ginger, washed
400g raw sugar
800g trimmed rhubarb, cut into
    3cm pieces

MAKES 500ML

DAIRY FREE
GLUTEN FREE
VEGETARIAN
VEGAN

QUICK FIX + CHILLING

1. Place lemon rind, orange rind, ginger and sugar in TC bowl, mill for 10 seconds, speed 9.
2. Add lemon juice, orange juice and rhubarb, cook for 20 minutes, 90°C, speed 1. Strain mixture through a fine sieve (see note). Refrigerate cordial until ready to serve.

TO SERVE

To serve, mix 1 part cordial to 6 parts soda water, still water or champagne and enjoy.

NOTE

Don't discard the rhubarb pulp – it makes a delicious breakfast topped with yoghurt and granola.

I cannot get enough of jams, chutneys and relishes – not only are they a great way to extend the life of seasonal produce, but they fit so perfectly with my 'favour makers' philosophy – always have things on hand to jazz up simple dishes. This one really is too easy to whip up, and incredibly cheap!

TOO EASY ONION JAM

6 brown onions, peeled and quartered
600g white or apple cider vinegar
300g raw sugar
½ teaspoon fine salt

MAKES 800ML

DAIRY FREE
GLUTEN FREE
VEGETARIAN
VEGAN

1. Place onions in TC bowl, chop for 10 seconds, speed 5.
2. Add remaining ingredients, cook for 1 hour, steaming temperature, reverse speed 2, MC removed and steamer basket on top to prevent splashes. Scrape down sides.
3. Cook for a further 5 minutes, steaming temperature, reverse speed 2, or until thick and jam consistency.
4. Spoon into warm, sterilised jars and store in the fridge for up to 6 months.

TO SERVE

Serve as a condiment with literally anything, or add a dollop to stews, soups, sauces and more for extra flavour.

It was my lovely staff member and friend Pauline who first introduced us to the wonders of real homemade piccalilli, and the whole office fell in love! It's a delicious chunky chutney with the perfect mix of sweet and tangy, combined with delicious spices. It's incredibly versatile so use whatever veggies are seasonal and plentiful, although cauliflower is my personal favourite.

PAULINE'S PICCALILLI

1kg mixed veggies, finely chopped – cauliflower, cucumber, carrots, capsicum, zucchini, shallots, green beans
50g fine salt
1 teaspoon cumin seeds
1 teaspoon coriander seeds
150g raw sugar
30g cornflour
50g Dijon mustard
2 teaspoons ground turmeric
60g apple cider vinegar

MAKES 1KG

DAIRY FREE
GLUTEN FREE
VEGETARIAN
VEGAN

1. Toss vegetables and salt together in a large bowl, then set aside overnight at room temperature.
2. The following day, place cumin and coriander seeds in TC bowl, mill for 2 seconds, speed 10.
3. Add sugar, cornflour, mustard, turmeric and vinegar, cook for 8 minutes, 90°C, speed 3.
4. Rinse veggies to remove salt and place in a large bowl. Pour over sauce and fold through to combine. Pack tightly into sterilised jars and seal.

TO SERVE

Store at room temperature and stand in a cool, dark place for a minimum 6 weeks before opening. Store in the fridge once opened. Serve on cheese boards, toss through salads, use as a sandwich filling or spread on toast.

This recipe was inspired by Tina, a passionate preserver who makes the most amazing chilli chutney. Of course, I just had to come up with my own thermo version! I have departed from the purist's recipe with the addition of a red capsicum. It's sweet and fiery and adds a great kick of flavour – a welcome departure from the usual tomato chutney. Chillies grow really well in small pots both indoors and out, so they are a really easy one to have at home. If I don't have 15 ready at the one time, I simply freeze them in a ziplock bag until I have enough.

CHILLI CHUTNEY

15 long red chillis, halved

1 red capsicum, quartered and seeds removed

2 Granny Smith apples, peeled, cored and quartered

200g raw sugar

100g apple cider vinegar

50g water

2 teaspoons fine salt

MAKES 2 CUPS

DAIRY FREE
GLUTEN FREE
VEGETARIAN
VEGAN

1. Place chilli, capsicum and apple in TC bowl, chop for 3 seconds, speed 6, assisting with spatula. Scrape down sides.
2. Add sugar, vinegar, water and salt, cook for 35 minutes, steaming temperature, reverse speed soft, MC removed and steamer basket on top to prevent splashes. Transfer chutney to warm, sterilised glass jars.

TO SERVE

Serve as a condiment with savoury pastries, eggs, grilled meats, or add to soups, stews and tomato-based sauces for a kick. Keep refrigerated for up to 6 months.

VARIATION

For a thinner sauce, cook for 30 rather than 35 minutes at step 2.

NOTE

For a milder chutney, deseed some or all of the chillies before cooking. Conversely, for a super fiery option, add a couple of bird's eye chillies in at step 1.

Keep lighter beetroots separate
to preserve their pretty hues.

If you like tinned beetroot slices, you'll love this recipe! The flavours are just so much better when they're homemade. I love keeping a stash in the fridge so I always have beetroot on hand.

'CANNED' BEETROOT

500g water

500g vinegar – white, malt or apple cider

40g raw sugar

2 tablespoons whole spices – peppercorns, mustard seeds, coriander seeds, cumin seeds, cloves, bay leaf

1 teaspoon fine salt

1kg beetroots, washed and ends trimmed (large or baby)

MAKES 2KG

DAIRY FREE
GLUTEN FREE
VEGETARIAN
VEGAN

1. Place water, vinegar, sugar, spices and salt in TC bowl. Place beetroot in steaming tray, steam for 30 minutes, steaming temperature, reverse speed 3, or until tender. Large beetroots will need 45 minutes.

2. Set beetroots aside for 10 minutes, or until cool enough to handle. Peel off beetroot skins by rubbing with fingers. Either slice beetroots or leave whole, then pack tightly into sterilised glass jars. Fill with vinegar mixture from TC bowl, completely submerging beetroot.

TO SERVE

Refrigerate for a minimum 1 week before enjoying. Keep for up to 6 months. Add to salads, burgers, sandwiches or grazing platters.

NOTE

If more liquid is needed to fully submerge beetroot, add extra vinegar and water (1:1 ratio).

Once all of your beetroots have been enjoyed, use the leftover liquid to pickle radishes, onions or cucumbers.

Trying to convince
my dad soup is a meal.

freezer friendly

The convenience the freezer offers is amazing, so make
sure it's always loaded up with delicious and nutritious
meals! While there isn't always time to cook a meal, there
is always time to defrost one, so with some careful planning
a homecooked meal is always at your fingertips. Autumn
is a great time to load the freezer up with bulk-cooked
dishes, as much of our favourite produce is at its best and
cheapest. I've included different serving suggestions for
many of the recipes, so the family will never know it's
the same dish on repeat.

This recipe makes a LOT! And that's precisely why I love it – I can stock the freezer with tasty and nourishing dinners to defrost throughout winter. While the thermo bowl can't cook a curry for twelve, it is the best sous chef, chopping, mixing and sautéing everything ready for the oven, making the whole recipe so simple and quick (in a roundabout way!). Pumpkins are at their absolute prime and cheapest in autumn and are the star ingredient in this curry, breaking down and slightly thickening the rich sauce.

PUMPKIN CURRY

2 brown onions, peeled and halved
8 garlic cloves, peeled
6cm piece ginger, peeled
200g red curry paste (see page 161)
80g tomato paste
50g coconut oil
800g coconut cream
100g stock concentrate (see page 249)
2kg pumpkin, peeled and cut into 3cm cubes
1kg potatoes, cut into 2cm cubes
1 red capsicum, cut into 2cm pieces
100g baby spinach leaves

SERVES 12

DAIRY FREE
GLUTEN FREE
VEGETARIAN
VEGAN

QUICK FIX + BAKING

1. Preheat oven to 170°C.
2. Place onion, garlic, ginger, curry paste, tomato paste and coconut oil in TC bowl, purée for 10 seconds, speed 8. Scrape down sides.
3. Sauté for 10 minutes, 100°C, speed 1.
4. Add coconut cream and stock concentrate, mix for 5 seconds, speed 4.
5. Place pumpkin and potato in a large casserole dish and pour over curry mixture. Cover and cook for 2 hours, or until pumpkin begins to break down and the potatoes are tender.
6. Add capsicum and spinach, stir to combine.

TO SERVE

Serve curry with steamed rice, roti bread or pappadums and garnish with lime wedges, coriander, mint, yoghurt, cashews or peanuts.

This is another one of my bulk-cook freezer options, making a huge pot of rich and smoky beans that can be served so many ways. This recipe does take a while (don't forget to soak your beans the day before!), but the actual hands-on time is minimal. I love the fact this recipe uses no cans, instead relying on fresh tomatoes and dried beans and lentils, just how nature intended.

CHILLI CON LENTIL

3 tablespoons cumin seeds
3 tablespoons coriander seeds
½ cinnamon stick
2 brown onions, peeled and halved
4 garlic cloves, peeled
2 long red chillies
50g olive oil
1kg ripe tomatoes, roughly chopped
100g tomato paste
30g golden syrup
3 tablespoons smoked paprika
½ teaspoon ground nutmeg
250g dried green lentils, rinsed
250g dried red lentils, rinsed
1.25 litres water
250g dried black beans, soaked in water for 24 hours
250g dried kidney beans, soaked in water for 24 hours
1 tablespoon fine salt

SERVES 12

DAIRY FREE
GLUTEN FREE
VEGETARIAN
VEGAN

1. Preheat oven to 160°C.
2. Place cumin, coriander and cinnamon in TC bowl, mill for 1 minute, speed 10.
3. Add onion, garlic and chilli, chop for 5 seconds, speed 5. Scrape down sides.
4. Add olive oil, sauté for 6 minutes, 100°C, speed 1.
5. Add tomatoes, tomato paste, golden syrup, paprika and nutmeg, chop for 8 seconds, speed 6.
6. Transfer mixture to a large casserole dish and add lentils and water. Drain beans, rinse, and add. Stir to combine. Cover with a tight-fitting lid and bake for 2½ hours, or until beans are tender. Stir through salt.

TO SERVE
Serve warm immediately, refrigerate for later or freeze in serving size containers.

NOTE
Make sure you give the beans plenty of water to soak in overnight as they will expand!

DINNER OPTIONS
Mexican fiesta: Chilli con lentil + corn chips + salsa + guacamole

Burrito bowl: Chilli con lentil + shredded lettuce + grated cheese + sour cream

Shepherd's pie: Chilli con lentil + mashed potato

This sauce is such a favourite of mine because it tastes rich, hearty and satisfying, but really it's all veggies! You would never guess the base was zucchini, carrot and mushrooms. Make this recipe throughout spring, summer and autumn, loading up the freezer to get you through winter, or whenever you need a quick meal. Heat up a container, cook some pasta and you've got the ultimate bowl food, faster than you could order takeout.

VEGETABLE BOLOGNAISE

2 garlic cloves, peeled

1 long red chilli (optional)

20g olive oil

2 carrots, cut into thirds

1 zucchini, cut into thirds

350g mushrooms, roughly
    chopped into 3cm pieces

90g black olives, pitted

30g miso paste (see note)

20g maple syrup

10g rice wine vinegar

1 tablespoon stock concentrate
    (see page 249)

½ teaspoon dried oregano

700g passata (see page 129)

SERVES 5

DAIRY FREE
GLUTEN FREE
VEGETARIAN
VEGAN

QUICK FIX

1. Place garlic and chilli in TC bowl, chop for 4 seconds, speed 6. Scrape down sides.

2. Add oil, cook for 5 minutes, 100°C, speed 1.

3. Add carrots, chop for 4 seconds, speed 5.

4. Add zucchini, chop for 3 seconds, speed 4.

5. Add mushrooms and olives, chop for 8 seconds, speed 3, assisting with spatula. Scrape down sides.

6. Add miso paste, maple syrup, vinegar, stock concentrate, oregano and passata, cook for 20 minutes, 90°C, reverse speed 2.

TO SERVE

Serve immediately, refrigerate for later or freeze in serving size containers to defrost later.

NOTE

I like to use red miso paste for this recipe, but whatever you have on hand is fine.

While I'd highly recommend homemade passata for this recipe, of course you can use a purchased bottle.

DINNER OPTIONS

Pasta bake: Vegetable bolognaise + lasagne sheets + cheese sauce

Light meal: Vegetable bolognaise + zucchini noodles

Veggie moussaka: Vegetable bolognaise + Grilled eggplant + béchamel sauce

This is one of Ellen's favourite soups to whip up, and I'm a big fan – so of course we had to share the recipe with you too! It's a quick-fix meal, full of fresh flavours while also creamy and nourishing. While there's absolutely no need to freeze it, I love the fact that it's a puréed soup meaning it's so easy to reheat, even if you've forgotten to defrost (see page 165 for instructions)! That's real fast food.

THAI RED LENTIL SOUP

1 brown onion, peeled and
    halved
20g olive oil
40g red curry paste (page 161)
300g split red lentils, rinsed just
    prior to cooking
750g water
250g coconut milk
1 lemongrass stalk, gently
    bashed with a rolling pin
4 fresh kaffir lime leaves
1 lime, juice only
20g tamari
½ teaspoon fine salt

SERVES 3

DAIRY FREE
GLUTEN FREE
VEGETARIAN
VEGAN

QUICK FIX

1. Place onion in TC bowl, chop for 5 seconds, speed 5. Scrape down sides.

2. Add oil and curry paste, sauté for 5 minutes, 100°C, speed 1.

3. Add lentils, water, coconut milk, lemongrass and kaffir lime leaves, cook for 17 minutes, 100°C, reverse speed 1.5.

4. Remove lemongrass and lime leaves. Add lime juice, tamari and salt, purée for 1 minute, speed 8 or until completely smooth.

TO SERVE

To serve, top with fresh coriander leaves and drizzle with chilli oil (page 37). To freeze, allow to cool completely before transferring to a shallow container.

NOTE

We like this soup thick, but it's very easy to add additional water or coconut milk to thin down if that's your preference (you could even stretch it to serve 4!).

I am such a fan of beef brisket – it may take forever to cook, but the resulting meat is melt-in-your-mouth tender and full of flavour, shredding up easily with a fork. Because it does take so long to cook, if I'm going to make it I always want to make a huge amount. Lucky it freezes well and can be served in so many different ways (and it's so delicious!).

MEXICAN BRISKET

2kg boneless grass-fed beef brisket

30g macadamia oil

1 brown onion, peeled and halved

6 garlic cloves, peeled

1kg ripe tomatoes, roughly chopped

60g stock concentrate (see page 249)

50g tomato paste

1 lime, juice only

40g Dijon mustard

20g golden syrup

1½ tablespoons smoked paprika

1 tablespoon ground cumin

2 teaspoons ground coriander

2 teaspoons ground chipotle chilli

SERVES 12

DAIRY FREE
GLUTEN FREE

1. Preheat oven to 200°C. Place meat in a large ovenproof dish (fattier side facing upwards) and rub with 10g of macadamia oil. Roast, uncovered, for 30 minutes.

2. Meanwhile, place onion and garlic in TC bowl, chop for 5 seconds, speed 5. Scrape down sides.

3. Add remaining 20g macadamia oil, sauté for 5 minutes, 100°C, speed 1.

4. Add tomatoes, stock concentrate, tomato paste, lime juice, mustard, golden syrup, smoked paprika, cumin, coriander and chipotle. Mix for 10 seconds, speed 8.

5. Cook for 10 minutes, 90°C, speed 1.

6. Reduce oven temperature to 140°C. Pour tomato mixture over the beef. Cover with a tight-fitting lid or multiple layers of foil and cook for a further 5 hours or until meltingly tender.

7. Remove meat from pan and shred using two large forks. Return meat back to the pan and stir through pan juices.

TO SERVE

You can serve immediately, although this dish always tastes better the next day! Refrigerate for up to 3 days or freeze in serving size containers.

DINNER OPTIONS

Tasty tacos: Mexican brisket + corn tortillas + shredded cabbage + sliced radishes + coriander

Hearty pasta: Mexican brisket + pappardelle + fresh parsley + grated parmesan

Texas sliders: Mexican brisket + bap rolls + coleslaw

The ultimate
vegetarian burger!

These patties taste just like your classic fast-food burger, but unbelievably they're made from eggplant! I was a sceptic too when Ellen first created the recipe, but now I am absolutely hooked, preferring these to the standard mincemeat option. This is such an easy way to cook with eggplant – no roasting required.

DIRTY BURGERS

80g macadamia nuts

100g good quality bread, halved and frozen

1 brown onion, peeled and halved

1 garlic clove, peeled

2 eggplants, roughly chopped (approx. 500g)

20g macadamia oil, plus extra for frying

1 large handful fresh parsley

3 tablespoons nutritional yeast flakes (see notes)

1 teaspoon fine salt

150g plain flour

SERVES 6

DAIRY FREE
VEGETARIAN
VEGAN

1. Place macadamia nuts and bread in TC bowl, mill for 8 seconds, speed 8. Remove from TC bowl and set aside.

2. Without cleaning TC bowl, add onion and garlic, chop for 5 seconds, speed 5. Scrape down sides.

3. Add eggplant and 20g macadamia oil, sauté for 20 minutes, steaming temperature, speed 2.

4. Add parsley, nutritional yeast flakes and salt, blend for 5 seconds, speed 6.

5. Add bread crumb mixture and flour, mix for 10 seconds, speed 3. Scrape down sides.

6. Mix for a further 5 seconds, speed 3. Using wet hands, form mixture into 6–8 patties.

7. Heat a liberal amount of macadamia oil in a large fry pan over medium heat. Once hot, add as many patties as will fit and cook for 3–5 minutes each side, or until golden brown. Repeat with remaining patties.

TO SERVE

Serve patties between a burger bun topped with tomato, lettuce, beetroot, pickles, cheese, mayonnaise, BBQ sauce, chutney or mustard. Alternatively, wrap uncooked patties and freeze for a quick meal another night.

NOTE

Nutritional yeast flakes are little yellow flakes full of B vitamins, minerals and protein with a surprisingly authentic cheese flavour! Available from health food stores. Not to be confused with baker's or brewer's yeast.

To cook frozen patties, heat macadamia oil in a large fry pan over medium heat. Once hot, add frozen patties and fry for 4–6 minutes each side, or until warmed through. No need to remember to defrost in advance!

Warning: these dumplings are addictive! I just love how something so moreish is actually predominantly cauliflower and other veggies. They're Loryn's creation, and the first time I tasted them I knew they were perfect for this book – utterly delicious, yet made with plenty of fresh ingredients. This recipe makes a huge batch, which is perfect because they freeze well and don't need to be defrosted before cooking – assuming of course you don't eat them all in one sitting like we do!

VEGGIE GYOZA

3cm piece ginger, peeled
3 garlic cloves, peeled
20g toasted sesame oil
400g cauliflower (approx. 400g), roughly chopped
360g extra firm tofu, chopped into 4cm cubes
2 small heads of boy choy, ends trimmed and halved
100g fresh shiitake mushrooms, halved
75g miso paste
25g tamari
15g maple syrup
3 teaspoons Chinese five spice powder
1 bunch spring onions, thinly sliced
80 gyoza or gow gee wrappers (approx. 2 packets)
Rice bran oil, for frying
Water (1–2 tablespoons)

MAKES 80

DAIRY FREE
VEGETARIAN
VEGAN

1. Place ginger and garlic in TC bowl, chop for 5 seconds, speed 5. Scrape down sides.

2. Add sesame oil, sauté for 5 minutes, 100°C, speed 1.

3. Add cauliflower, tofu, bok choy and mushrooms, mince for 10 seconds, speed 4, assisting with spatula.

4. Add miso paste, tamari, maple syrup and five spice powder, cook for 8 minutes, 100°C, reverse speed 2, MC removed.

5. Fold through spring onions using a spatula, mixing the bottom mixture to the top.

6. Place 1 heaped teaspoon of filling in the middle of a gyoza wrapper and fold in half. Seal by pinching the edges together. Repeat with remaining mixture.

7. Heat enough oil in large fry pan to just cover the base on medium heat. Arrange the dumplings in the pan and cook for 3–5 minutes, or until the base is golden brown.

8. Add 1–2 tablespoons of water depending on the size of your pan, then immediately cover with a lid. Cook for 5 minutes then check to see if dumplings are cooked and all water has evaporated. Remove dumplings from pan and repeat with remaining dumplings, adding additional oil each time.

TO SERVE

Serve with peanut dipping sauce (page 49), Chinese vinegar or sriracha chilli sauce, and garnish with spring onions or sesame seeds.

NOTE

To freeze, complete steps 1–6 and then freeze uncooked dumplings in a single layer, ensuring they don't touch. Once frozen you can combine them all in a large container or ziplock bag. When ready to cook, resume from step 6 using the frozen dumplings. Cook for 8 minutes rather than 5 at step 8.

Toss curry paste with soba noodles for a quick and tasty meal.

If you're shopping for this recipe, how about making a batch of red curry paste also – the ingredients are almost the same, saving you time and money. And you'll thank yourself later when the freezer is stocked and a delicious and nutritious meal is only a handful of ingredients away!

GREEN CURRY PASTE

1 tablespoon toasted coriander seeds
1 teaspoon toasted cumin seeds
½ teaspoon white peppercorns
2 teaspoons fine salt
1 lime, rind and juice
12 long green chillies
2 red Asian shallots, peeled and halved
12 garlic cloves, peeled
1cm piece galangal, peeled
1 lemongrass stalk, white part only, cut into 1cm pieces
2 fresh coriander roots with stems and leaves
80g coconut oil

MAKES 1½ CUPS

DAIRY FREE
GLUTEN FREE
VEGETARIAN
VEGAN

QUICK FIX

1. Place coriander seeds, cumin seeds, peppercorns and salt in TC bowl, mill for 10 seconds, speed 8.
2. Add lime rind, mill for 8 seconds, speed 8.
3. Add chillies, shallots, garlic, galangal, lemongrass, coriander, lime juice and coconut oil, purée for 12 seconds, speed 7. Scrape down sides and lid.
4. Sauté for 10 minutes, 100°C, speed 1.
5. Purée 1 minute, speed 5.

STORAGE

Place in a sterilised jar or freeze in ice cube trays.

NOTE

For a milder curry, remove the seeds and membrane from the chillies first.

DINNER OPTIONS

Colourful noodles: Green curry paste + toasted sesame oil + noodles + spiralised carrot and zucchini

Spicy prawns: Green curry paste + coconut oil + prawns

Classic curry: Green curry paste + coconut milk + veggies

*I always freeze
my curry pastes
in ice trays.*

I think of homemade curry pastes as short-term pain, long-term gain – while the ingredient list is slightly overwhelming, I know I'll be making delicious meals for months to come with minimal effort once I've got this flavoursome paste stashed in the freezer!

RED CURRY PASTE

2 teaspoons toasted coriander
    seeds
1 teaspoon toasted cumin seeds
2 teaspoons white peppercorns
2 teaspoons fine salt
1 lime, rind only
8 long fresh red chillies
3 red Asian shallots, peeled and
    halved
12 garlic cloves, peeled
3cm piece galangal, peeled
2 lemongrass stalks, white part
    only, cut into 1cm pieces
2 coriander roots with stems
1 teaspoon ground turmeric
1 teaspoon sweet paprika
80g coconut oil

MAKES 1½ CUPS

DAIRY FREE
GLUTEN FREE
VEGETARIAN
VEGAN

QUICK FIX

1. Place coriander seeds, cumin seeds, peppercorns and salt in TC bowl, mill for 10 seconds, speed 8.
2. Add lime rind, mill for 8 seconds, speed 8.
3. Add chillies, shallots, garlic, galangal, lemongrass, coriander, turmeric, paprika and coconut oil, purée for 12 seconds, speed 7. Scrape down sides and lid.
4. Sauté for 8 minutes, 100°C, speed 1.
5. Purée for 1 minute, speed 5.

STORAGE

Place in a sterilised jar or freeze in ice cube trays.

NOTE

For a milder curry, remove seeds and membrane from chillies before using.

DINNER OPTIONS

Creamy laksa: Red curry paste + coconut milk + noodles + prawns + veggies

Thai pumpkin soup: Red curry paste + pumpkin soup

Spicy mussels: Red curry paste + stock + fresh mussels + lime juice + toasted baguette

FRESH TO FREEZER

I love loading up the freezer with plenty of meals ready to defrost in an instant, meaning I've always got something homemade and delicious at my fingertips, even if I don't have time to cook (or need a night off!). This way there's never a need for takeaway, and I can enjoy all the beautiful summer and autumn produce throughout the colder months. Here's my tips for freezer-meal domination:

LIQUIDS
Puréed sauces, soups and stocks:

- **Stick to shallow plastic.** When freezing soups and stocks I always stick to plastic containers to avoid the possibility of broken glass, as liquid expands when freezing. Shallow containers are the best choice as it makes it easiest to remove the frozen block when you're ready to reheat.

- **No need to defrost.** Puréed soups are the easiest of freezer dinners, because they are just so quick to defrost and reheat with the thermo cooker. When ready to eat, pop the frozen soup block out of the container, then use a large knife to cut into chunks, just as you would when re-emulsifying sorbet or ice-cream (no need to defrost first!). Transfer to TC bowl, blitz for 10 seconds, speed 9, then warm for 10 minutes, 100°C, speed 2, or until soup is heated to your liking. Easy as that! If you have already defrosted your liquid in the fridge and are just needing to reheat, skip the blitz step.

IN-BETWEENS
Curries, ragus, bakes, pasta, chunky soups and sauces:

- **The smaller the container, the better.** Freeze meals in portions that you and your family will eat in one sitting. Then you can simply defrost the amount you want, not the whole batch! If in doubt, you're better freezing in multiple small containers.

- **Preparation is key.** Ideally, pull out your frozen dinner the night before or that morning and allow to defrost in the fridge. By dinnertime your meal should be defrosted and ready to reheat – this will save you a lot of time in the evening!

- **Saved by the steam.** If you haven't defrosted your meal come dinnertime, move over microwave – use your steaming tray! Much gentler and healthier. Place your frozen meal inside a glass container or casserole dish with a lid and sit inside the steaming tray. If your dish is covering all the steaming holes, you'll need to place two crossed forks in the bottom of the tray to elevate the dish. Place 500g water in TC bowl and steam for 20 minutes, steaming temperature, speed 3, or until defrosted. Once defrosted you can keep steaming to reheat your meal, just ensure to add more water if steaming for longer than 30 minutes.

Did you know you
can freeze bagels?
Recipe page 195.

SOLIDS

Dumplings, steamed buns, meatballs, gnocchi, pastries, breads and bagels:

- **Freeze flat.** It's important when freezing solid items that they aren't touching each other as they freeze. Line a baking tray with a baking mat or baking paper and place individual items close together but not touching. Place in freezer. After eight hours you can transfer your frozen goods to a container or ziplock bag – once they're frozen solid they're very robust with no risk of sticking together. The exception is baked goods such as bagels and bread rolls, which can be thrown straight in a ziplock bag with no need to freeze flat first.

- **Straight from the freezer.** When reheating solid items, there's no need to defrost first! Put dumplings, gyoza, steamed buns, gnocchi and meatballs straight on the steaming tray, fill TC bowl with 500g water and steam for 15 minutes, or until defrosted and heated through.

- **In the oven for baked goods.** Still no need to defrost first, but baked goods such as pastries, breads and bagels need the dry heat of the oven rather than the steam. Place frozen goods in a preheated 180°C oven until defrosted through (and possibly warmed also!).

WINTER

More time indoors means more time in the kitchen! Now's the time to get baking, filling the house with the warming aromas of freshly baked bread and sugar and spice and all things nice. As the mornings become cold and dark, a warm and satisfying breakfast takes on a whole new importance to me. Hearty and comforting meals also become a focus, and while the cooler weather may not offer as much variety as the warmer months, there's certainly still plenty of delicious produce to choose from.

My favourite winter produce:

Apple	Mandarin
Avocado	Nashi
Broccoli	Orange
Brussels sprouts	Pear
Carrot	Rosemary
Cumquat	Salad greens
Kohlrabi	Silverbeet
Leek	Tangelo

hearty & comforting

Sometimes you just need a big bowl of comfort food,
and these dishes are some of my absolute favourites!
Rich and satisfying, while still celebrating fresh and
flavoursome produce. I've got super quick-fix options
for mid-week, but also show stoppers for when something
a little more special is in order. So throw out those takeaway
menus and make all those moreish foods yourself, from
pasta and pizza to curry — there's a dish in here that's sure
to impress your audience and cure your craving.

*I love a really simple sauce
like burnt sage butter.*

This recipe is not my usual quick-fix meal, but boy is it worth the extra effort! The soft, pillowy gnocchi is the stuff of food dreams. Everyone will be so impressed you made it yourself from scratch, it might just become your entertaining go-to (it's one of mine!). I promise it's not as difficult as you might think, especially with the thermo doing the brunt of the technical stuff.

POTATO GNOCCHI

1kg red potatoes, peeled and quartered
400g plain flour, plus extra for rolling
2 free-range eggs
2 pinches fine salt
700g water

SERVES 6

DAIRY FREE
VEGETARIAN

1. Place 800g water in TC bowl. Place potatoes in lower steaming tray and steam for 30 minutes, steaming temperature, speed 3. Refrigerate potatoes until cool and you are ready to make the dough.

2. Place 200g flour, half the cold potatoes, 1 egg and 1 pinch of salt in TC bowl, mix 10 seconds, speed 6.

3. Knead for 12 seconds, interval speed. Tip onto a lightly floured surface.

4. Repeat with remaining flour, potato, egg and salt.

5. Combine doughs and gently knead into a disc shape, adding flour if sticky but with caution – too much flour makes the gnocchi tough.

6. Cut off 3cm strips of dough and roll each piece into a rope, 2cm in diameter. Cut into 2cm pieces with a dough cutter or butter knife. Indent each piece in the middle with your thumb and squeeze lightly together.

7. Place water in TC bowl, heat for 8 minutes, steaming temperature, speed 3, or until steaming temperature is reached. Meanwhile, place wet baking paper in both the lower steaming tray and upper steaming tray. Place gnocchi pieces on the baking paper making sure they don't touch.

8. Steam gnocchi for 6 minutes, steaming temperature, speed 3, or until cooked through. Repeat with remaining gnocchi.

TO SERVE
Keep gnocchi warm until ready to serve or heat macadamia oil in a large fry pan over medium heat and lightly fry gnocchi until golden. Serve with any pasta sauce.

NOTE
You can freeze cooked gnocchi and either defrost or reheat in the thermo steaming tray or in a fry pan – a great option for getting organised in advance when entertaining.

Definitely one of my more unusual creations, but one of my favourites! Especially for the cooler months. Think of a rich and creamy peanut curry, combined with soft and pillowy balls of mashed potato and a crispy fried coating. I love this recipe when I'm entertaining as it easily suits a wide variety of eating preferences – serve it with a big bowl of steamed rice, roasted cauliflower and sliced cucumber and you've got yourself an easy Indian banquet.

POTATO DUMPLINGS IN CREAMY CURRY

1 litre water

1kg Russet potatoes, peeled and roughly cut into 3cm pieces

100g plain flour

200g frozen peas, defrosted

1½ teaspoons fine salt

2 tablespoons coconut oil

1 brown onion, peeled and halved

3 garlic cloves, peeled

50g red curry paste (see page 161)

400g can coconut cream

50g natural peanut butter

20g stock concentrate (see page 249)

1 teaspoon ground turmeric

SERVES 5

DAIRY FREE
GLUTEN FREE (OPTION)
VEGETARIAN
VEGAN

1. Fill TC bowl with the water. Place potatoes in lower steaming tray and steam for 30 minutes, steaming temperature, speed 3, or until soft and cooked through. Set aside.

2. Place cooked potatoes in a dry TC bowl, mash for 10 seconds, speed 6, or until smooth.

3. Add flour, peas and 1 teaspoon salt, knead for 20 seconds, dough function, or until a soft dough is formed. Roll dough into roughly 20 golf-ball sized balls – if sticky, flour hands first.

4. Heat oil over medium heat in a large fry pan. Fry balls for 10 minutes, rotating often, until browned all over.

5. Meanwhile, place onion and garlic in TC bowl, chop for 5 seconds, speed 5. Scrape down sides.

6. Add curry paste, sauté for 5 minutes, 100°C, speed 1.

7. Add coconut cream, peanut butter, stock concentrate, turmeric and remaining salt, cook for 6 minutes, 100°C, speed 2.

TO SERVE

Pour curry sauce into a wide, shallow bowl and top with warm potato dumplings. Serve immediately with rice, roti bread or roasted cauliflower.

VARIATION

For a gluten-free option, use gluten-free flour. While peanut butter is my pick for this recipe, if peanuts are an issue substitute with almond or cashew butter, or simply leave out altogether.

I've got my thermo cooker bolognaise sauce down to an art form. It can be easy to over-process the meat and end up with a watery sauce, but my mum Janene has developed the perfect recipe, so fear not! We are sure it will become a favourite, with love from our family to yours.

SPAGHETTI BOLOGNAISE

2 brown onions, peeled and halved

2 garlic cloves, peeled

100g mushrooms (halved if large)

40g olive oil

400g can diced tomatoes

200g tomato paste

80g red wine

50g stock concentrate (see page 249)

40g balsamic reduction (see note)

1 teaspoon dried oregano

3 sprigs rosemary, leaves only

1 teaspoon fine salt

600g full-fat grass-fed beef mince, roughly crumbled

500g spaghetti

SERVES 5

DAIRY FREE

QUICK FIX

1. Place onion and garlic in TC bowl, chop for 4 seconds, speed 5.
2. Add mushrooms, chop 3 seconds, speed 5. Scrape down sides.
3. Add oil, sauté for 5 minutes, 100°C, reverse speed 1.
4. Add diced tomatoes, tomato paste, red wine, stock concentrate, balsamic reduction, oregano, rosemary and salt, cook for 5 minutes, 100°C speed 1.
5. Add beef to TC bowl, cook for 10 minutes, 100°C, reverse speed 1.5.
6. Meanwhile, cook pasta on stove according to packet directions, then drain.

TO SERVE

Spoon sauce over cooked pasta and serve. (Or save the sauce and eat it the next day – it tastes even better!)

NOTE

Balsamic reduction is a sweeter, thicker, condensed form of balsamic vinegar. My recipe can be found in *Everyday Thermo Cooking*, but you can also buy premade versions at good delicatessens.

VARIATION

If available, top with fresh cherry tomatoes, basil and grated cheese.

One of my all-time favourite flavour combinations.

This is a lavish dish, really set to impress! Invite people over and take your time to enjoy with a glass of Shiraz. The polenta base is a rich and creamy version of the classic pizza base, but will start to crisp up around the edges in the oven. It perfectly matches the richness of the mushrooms and blue cheese, while the walnuts add crunch and the rocket and balsamic add freshness. The whole recipe is conveniently gluten free and vegetarian, but you wouldn't know it's missing a thing.

POLENTA PIZZA

1 litre water

50g stock concentrate (see page 249)

1 teaspoon salt, plus extra, to taste

200g fine yellow cornmeal

Macadamia oil, for drizzling

500g baby Swiss brown mushrooms, halved

50g rocket

100g gorgonzola, crumbled (or any cheese)

80g walnuts

Balsamic reduction, for drizzling (see note)

SERVES 6

GLUTEN FREE
VEGETARIAN

1. Insert butterfly in TC bowl. Add water, stock concentrate and salt, heat for 12 minutes, 100°C, speed 3. During the last 2 minutes, slowly add cornmeal through the hole in the lid.

2. Cook for 10 minutes, 80°C, speed soft. Line a large baking tray with baking paper (approx. 30 x 40cm). Pour polenta onto lined tray and spread out evenly using a knife or spatula — it should be approx. 1.5cm thick. Allow to cool completely (you can refrigerate up for to 24 hours).

3. Preheat oven to 200°C. Brush polenta base with macadamia oil and bake for 40 minutes or until beginning to crisp up around the edges.

4. Meanwhile, toss mushrooms with a drizzle of macadamia oil and a pinch of salt. When polenta has been baking for 20 minutes, add mushrooms to oven and roast for 20 minutes or until tender.

TO SERVE

Just prior to serving, top polenta base with roasted mushrooms, rocket, gorgonzola and walnuts, then drizzle with balsamic reduction. Use a large flat-blade knife to cut into slices and use a spatula to serve onto plates.

NOTE

I have a recipe for balsamic reduction in *Everyday Thermo Cooking* or pick up a bottle from your local supermarket or delicatessen.

I absolutely love this recipe – not only because it uses mussels, one of my favourite ingredients, but because the entire thing, start to finish, is done in the thermo in under 30 minutes! No pots, pans or stovetop required. To my mind, mussels are the ultimate modern protein source – sustainable, ethical, locally produced, require no feed inputs as they filter food from the surrounding water, cheap, quick to cook and of course they are really tasty! I believe I could make a mussel convert out of anyone, and this recipe is no exception – creamy garlicky spaghetti, flavoursome mussels, chives and a kick of chilli if you want it!

ONE-BOWL MUSSEL SPAGHETTI

1 brown onion, peeled and halved

3 garlic cloves, peeled

50g olive oil

600g water

100g white wine or cider

100g pouring cream

50g stock concentrate (see page 249)

1 teaspoon fine salt

1kg mussels, scrubbed and debearded

400g spaghetti, broken in half

1 bunch black kale, spines removed, leaves very finely chopped

1 bunch chives, finely chopped

Chilli flakes, to serve (optional)

SERVES 4

QUICK FIX

1. Place onion and garlic in TC bowl, chop for 5 seconds, speed 5. Scrape down sides.

2. Add oil, sauté for 5 minutes, 100°C, speed 1.

3. Add water, wine or cider, cream, stock concentrate and salt. Place mussels in lower steaming tray. Steam for 13 minutes, steaming temperature, reverse speed 3.

4. Remove steaming tray and set aside. (Mussels should now be cooked. If they aren't, steam for a further 2 minutes, steaming temperature, speed 3, or until cooked.) Add spaghetti through hole in TC lid. Cook for 6 minutes, 100°C, reverse speed soft.

5. Add kale and gently combine with spaghetti, folding the top spaghetti to the bottom. Replace lid and leave standing for 10 minutes in the TC bowl to complete cooking.

TO SERVE

Divide pasta and broth between 4 serving bowls, top with mussels and garnish with chives and chilli flakes if desired.

Creamy and satisfying, chock-full of veggies and ready in just over 20 minutes, this recipe ticks all my boxes! It's a great one to have up your sleeve for quick dinners – I often have the fresh ingredients on hand from my weekly produce delivery.

CREAMY CAULIFLOWER SOUP

1 brown onion, peeled and halved

4 garlic cloves, peeled

3cm piece ginger, peeled

1 long red chilli, halved

1 tablespoon curry powder

40g coconut oil

600g cauliflower, cut into chunks

1 carrot, quartered

400g coconut milk

200g water

50g stock concentrate (see page 249)

SERVES 4

DAIRY FREE
GLUTEN FREE
VEGETARIAN
VEGAN

QUICK FIX

1. Place onion, garlic, ginger and chilli in TC bowl, chop for 6 seconds, speed 5. Scrape down sides.

2. Add curry powder and coconut oil, sauté for 5 minutes, 100°C, speed 1.

3. Add cauliflower and carrot, grate for 5 seconds, speed 8.

4. Add coconut milk, water and stock concentrate, cook for 15 minutes, 100°C, speed 2.

5. Purée for 30 seconds, speed 9.

TO SERVE

Divide soup between 4 serving bowls. Optional toppings: coriander, garlic crumbs (page 41), fresh chilli or fried chickpeas.

NOTE

This soup freezes really well. Follow the steps on page 165 to defrost and reheat.

My team cannot get enough of these moreish 'sausage' rolls! The mushrooms are so meaty and flavoursome, no one's missing the mince. We love these for a casual dinner paired with a delicious chilli chutney (page 139) and side salad, but they also make great finger food when entertaining. Let's be honest, anything wrapped in pastry is a crowd pleaser!

MINI MUSHROOM 'SAUSAGE' ROLLS

Handful fresh parsley, leaves only

120g bread (preferably sourdough), roughly chopped and frozen

1 brown onion, peeled and halved

3 garlic cloves, peeled

40g olive oil

500g Swiss brown mushrooms, roughly chopped

25g balsamic reduction (see note on page 175)

1 teaspoon fine salt

3 sheets puff pastry

MAKES 12

DAIRY FREE (OPTION)
VEGETARIAN
VEGAN (OPTION)

NOTE

You can refrigerate the mushroom mixture for up to 48 hours, so it's a handy one to get started on early when entertaining.

1. Place parsley and bread in TC bowl, mill for 10 seconds, speed 8. Remove from the TC bowl and set aside.

2. Place onion and garlic in TC bowl, chop for 5 seconds, speed 5. Scrape down sides.

3. Add oil, sauté for 5 minutes, 100°C, speed 1.

4. Add mushrooms, chop for 10 seconds, speed 4, assisting with spatula.

5. Add balsamic reduction and salt, cook for 10 minutes, steaming temperature, speed 1, MC removed and steamer basket on top to prevent splashes.

6. Add breadcrumb mixture, fold through using spatula. Refrigerate for a minimum 1 hour.

7. When ready to cook, preheat oven to 200°C.

8. Place a third of the chilled mixture along the edge of a pastry sheet and roll to form a log. Cut into quarters with a serrated knife. Place seam-side down on a baking tray lined with baking paper. Repeat with remaining mixture.

9. Bake rolls for 25 minutes or until browned.

TO SERVE

Serve hot out of the oven with tomato or chilli chutney (see page 139) or allow to cool completely before packing into lunchboxes.

VARIATION

For a dairy-free and vegan option, ensure your pastry is isn't butter puff pastry.

Sprinkle with sesame seeds prior to baking (pictured).

This dish is so impressive, yet foolproof! People often struggle cooking fish, but I promise this recipe couldn't be simpler. The whiting simply melts in your mouth while the cream sauce is rich and buttery, with just enough citrus to cut through. Whiting is one of only a handful of fillet fish that is considered a sustainable choice by the Australian Marine Conservation Society, so skip the salmon and give this dish a go – you won't be disappointed!

WHITING IN CREAMY LEMON SAUCE

1 lemon, rind only
2 garlic cloves, peeled
80g thickened cream
40g butter
30g Dijon mustard
½ teaspoon fine salt
4 whiting fillets, skinless and
   boneless (approx. 400g)

SERVES 4

GLUTEN FREE

QUICK FIX

1. Preheat oven to 200°C.
2. Place lemon rind and garlic in TC bowl, chop for 10 seconds, speed 8. Scrape down sides.
3. Add cream, butter, mustard and salt, cook for 5 minutes, 80°C, speed 3.
4. Lay fish fillets flat in a large roasting dish. Pour over cream sauce and bake for 12 minutes, or until fish is just cooked.

TO SERVE

Garnish with parsley, dill, tarragon, lemon slices or paprika, and serve with steamed rice, mashed potato, roasted potato, steamed greens or crusty sourdough bread to mop up all of the delicious sauce.

Everyone will be eating Brussels sprouts with this recipe! The garlic crumb is crunchy, cheesy and golden, while the sprouts are tender and caramelised. Not a bitter or limp veggie in sight! Technically I suppose this is a side dish, but honestly, I'd be very happy with a big bowl of just these sprouts for dinner.

GARLIC CRUMBED SPROUTS

4 garlic cloves, peeled
1 lemon, rind only
150g parmesan cheese
1 teaspoon fine salt
200g sourdough bread, roughly chopped and frozen
1kg Brussels sprouts, halved
40g macadamia oil

SERVES 8

VEGETARIAN

QUICK FIX + ROASTING

1. Preheat oven to 180°C.
2. Place garlic, lemon rind, cheese and salt in TC bowl, chop for 2 seconds, speed 8.
3. Add bread, mill for 10 seconds, speed 8. Transfer crumb mixture to 2 large roasting trays.
4. Without cleaning TC bowl, fill with 500g water. Place Brussels sprouts in lower steaming tray, steam for 12 minutes, steaming temperature, speed 3.
5. Toss sprouts in macadamia oil, then transfer to roasting trays and toss in crumb mixture. Roast for 20 minutes, or until Brussels sprouts are starting to crisp on the outside and crumb mixture is golden.

TO SERVE
Enjoy straight from the oven when the sprouts and crumbs are hot and crunchy.

These potatoes are the absolute best – soft and fluffy on the inside, crispy and golden on the outside, and with just the right amount of chilli and spice. Everyone will want seconds!

CRISPY SPICED POTATOES

500g water

1kg chat potatoes, halved

3 garlic cloves, peeled

70g macadamia oil

2 teaspoons black mustard seeds

2 teaspoons garam masala

1 teaspoon fine salt

½ teaspoon chilli powder

SERVES 4

DAIRY FREE
GLUTEN FREE
VEGETARIAN
VEGAN

QUICK FIX + ROASTING

1. Preheat oven and a large baking tray to 210°C.
2. Fill TC bowl with the water and place potatoes in lower steaming tray. Steam for 18 minutes, steaming temperature, speed 3, or until tender. Set aside.
3. Place garlic in dry TC bowl. Chop for 5 seconds, speed 5.
4. Add macadamia oil, mustard seeds, garam masala, salt and chilli powder, heat for 1 minute, 60°C, speed 2.
5. Add potatoes, mix for 5 seconds, reverse speed 4.
6. Tip potato mixture onto hot baking tray, spread out evenly and roast for 25 minutes, or until potatoes are golden and crunchy.

TO SERVE

Serve hot straight out of the oven. For something different, serve these potatoes alongside a curry instead of the usual rice or bread.

bake it 'til you make it

I love baking, especially in the cooler months – it makes the whole house seem warm and cozy. Perhaps it's the radiating oven, but I think more likely it's the heavenly aromas. Winter produce lends itself beautifully to baked creations – I love making fruits and vegetables the star of most of these baked recipes, extending the celebrations of fresh produce to carrot cake, olive bread and apple pie.

One more for me!

I love making my own bagels, and have done right from my earliest thermo cooker days! Steaming them is so much easier than boiling, and the results are just perfection. Here I've used a mix of standard bread flour and spelt flour, which adds to the flavour and also to the nutritional profile. While most breads require a 30-minute cool-down period before slicing, bagels are one of the few exceptions where you can tuck straight in without reproach! So enjoy.

CINNAMON RAISIN BAGELS

130g raw sugar, plus extra to
     sprinkle
1 cinnamon stick
430g litres water
2 teaspoons dried yeast
600g white baker's flour
100g wholemeal spelt flour
1 teaspoon fine salt
150g raisins
Oil, for proving bowl

MAKES 12

DAIRY FREE
VEGETARIAN
VEGAN

VARIATION

You can use regular wholemeal flour or rye flour instead of spelt.

1. Place sugar and cinnamon stick in TC bowl, mill for 1 minute, speed 10.

2. Add water and yeast, heat for 2 minutes, 37°C, speed 2.

3. Add flours and salt, mix for 6 seconds, speed 6.

4. Add raisins, knead for 90 seconds, interval speed, or until dough comes together and raisins are incorporated. You may need to add a tablespoon more of either flour or water if the dough is too sticky or too dry.

5. Place dough in an oiled bowl, cover and stand in a warm place for 1 hour, or until doubled in size.

6. Preheat oven to 180°C. Cut 12 squares of baking paper just larger than a bagel.

7. Divide mixture into 12 and shape into balls on a floured surface, rolling to create as tight a ball as possible. Press thumb through the middle of each ball and shape into bagels, placing each on their own piece of baking paper.

8. Place 800g water in TC bowl, heat for 7 minutes, steaming temperature, speed 3, or until steaming temperature is reached.

9. Place 4 bagels (on baking paper) on upper steaming tray and 2 bagels on lower steaming tray. Steam for 4 minutes, steaming temperature, speed 3. Transfer to baking tray, using the corners of the baking paper to lift. Repeat with remaining 6 bagels.

10. Lightly spray bagels with water and sprinkle with extra sugar. Bake for 20 minutes, or until browned with a crusty top and bottom.

TO SERVE

Enjoy warm straight out of the oven with lashings of butter.

These sweet and spicy cookies are dead easy – no worrying about whether the dough is too warm or too cold. Just plonk spoonfuls on the baking tray and you're set! With a well-stocked pantry you'll likely have all the ingredients on hand, making this recipe a handy one to have up your sleeve. And no one would ever guess you've used the healthier wholemeal spelt flour rather the usual plain flour!

GINGERBREAD SPELT COOKIES

75g brown sugar

1 cinnamon stick

4 cloves

75g butter

50g golden syrup

1 free-range egg

150g wholemeal spelt flour

2 teaspoons ground ginger

1 teaspoon vanilla extract

½ teaspoon bicarbonate of soda

Pinch salt

MAKES 18

VEGETARIAN

QUICK FIX

1. Preheat oven to 170°C.

2. Place sugar, cinnamon and cloves in TC bowl, mill for 30 seconds, speed 10.

3. Add butter and golden syrup, melt for 3 minutes, 60°C, speed 3.

4. Add egg, flour, ginger, vanilla extract, bicarbonate of soda and salt, mix for 10 seconds, speed 3. Scrape down sides and mix for a further 5 seconds.

5. Line 2 oven trays with baking paper or silicone baking mats and place heaped tablespoons of mixture well-spaced out on trays. Bake for 10 minutes, or until slightly puffed and golden in colour. Allow cookies to cool before removing from tray.

TO SERVE

Store completely cooled cookies in an airtight container and enjoy with a cup of tea.

You are going to love this cake – not only is it moist and delicious, but it's wheat free, dairy free, egg free, nut free, vegan and it contains four whole apples! You could even eat it for breakfast. It takes next to no time to whip up the batter as the thermo cooker swiftly takes care of grating all those apples and there's no separating eggs, sifting flour or creaming butter – my kind of baking.

SPICED APPLE CAKE

20g flaxseeds

75g water

4 apples, quartered and cored (about 650g, see note)

150g raw sugar

100g golden syrup

200g almond milk, soy milk or macadamia milk

150g macadamia oil, coconut oil or light olive oil, plus extra for greasing

300g spelt flour

1½ teaspoons bicarbonate of soda

1 teaspoon baking powder

1 teaspoon mixed spice

¼ teaspoon fine salt

1. Preheat oven to 175°C. Grease and line a 24cm springform pan with baking paper.
2. Place flaxseeds in TC bowl, mill for 10 seconds, speed 9. Transfer to a small bowl along with water, set aside.
3. Without cleaning TC bowl, add apples, chop for 10 seconds, speed 4.
4. Add sugar, golden syrup, milk, oil, flour, bicarbonate of soda, baking powder, mixed spice, salt and flaxseed mixture, mix for 10 seconds, reverse speed 3. Scrape down sides.
5. Mix for a further 4 seconds, reverse speed 3. Transfer mixture to prepared pan and bake for 1 hour, or until a skewer inserted comes out clean.

TO SERVE

Allow to cool before removing from pan. Once cool, liberally ice with friendly frosting (page 212, pictured).

SERVES 12

DAIRY FREE
VEGETARIAN
VEGAN

QUICK FIX + BAKING

NOTE

You can use any apples you like for this cake, but I like to go with a mix of sweet and sour apples such as Pink Ladies or Royal Galas and Granny Smiths.

While spelt flour has a much lower gluten content than standard wheat flour, it still does contain a small amount of gluten, so may be a problem for some people.

My mum has been crafting this recipe for years, intent on a fresher take on the classic by not pre-cooking the filling. The result is decadent without being overly sweet or heavy, allowing the apples to really shine. There are a few more steps than most of my recipes, but the thermo cooker does save you significant time over the conventional method – and homemade pastry is the best!

APPLE PIE WITH FLAKY PASTRY

340g plain flour, plus extra for dusting

120g raw sugar, plus extra for sprinkling

1¼ teaspoons fine salt

230g cold butter, cut into 2cm cubes

150g chilled water

1 lemon, rind and juice (approx. ½ rind, 30g juice)

2 tablespoons cornflour

1.1kg Granny Smith apples peeled, cored and quartered

½ teaspoon ground cinnamon

120g sultanas

1 free-range egg, lightly beaten

MAKES 1 PIE

VEGETARIAN

1. Place flour, 20g sugar, 1 teaspoon salt and 170g butter in TC bowl, mix for 10 seconds, speed 4.
2. Add water, knead for 30 seconds, dough function. Scrape down sides.
3. Knead for a further 10 seconds, dough function.
4. Tip onto a baking mat or a piece of baking paper and shape into a disc, incorporating the crumbly edges until all combined. If not coming together, spray once with water to complete shaping. Wrap in baking mat or paper and set aside in fridge.
5. Meanwhile, place lemon rind and cornflour in clean TC bowl, mill for 10 seconds, speed 9.
6. Add 550g apples, cinnamon, 100g sugar, lemon juice, ¼ teaspoon salt and 50g butter, chop for 4 seconds, speed 4. Set aside.
7. Place remaining 550g apple in TC bowl, chop for 4 seconds, speed 4. Add to apple mixture, add sultanas and fold everything together using a spatula.
8. Preheat oven to 190°C using the pastry-bake or bottom heat option if available.

continued ⟶

9. Remove pastry from fridge, cut off 430g pastry and return remaining pastry to fridge. Lightly flour your work surface and start to roll your pastry from the middle to the outside, moving the pastry after every 2–3 rolls to make sure it isn't sticking to your surface. Dust with extra flour if necessary. You're aiming for a round of pastry 4mm thick. Line a 25cm pie dish with the pastry, then trim the edges leaving a 2cm overhang.

10. Remove remaining pastry from fridge and roll out as before. Add apple mixture to pie dish and use the back of a spoon to push down on the apple, packing it tightly. Position pastry top and use a fork to press down on the edges to crimp together, dipping the fork into flour to prevent it from sticking. Trim overhanging pastry. Use leftover pastry pieces to cut out shapes for decorating the top of your pie.

11. Add shapes to decorate, brush pie top with beaten egg and sprinkle all over with extra raw sugar. Use a sharp knife to make 4 slits in the top to allow steam to escape while cooking and pierce several holes in the top with a skewer.

12. Bake for 50 minutes, rotating if necessary to ensure even cooking. If the edges are beginning to brown too quickly, cover with foil.

TO SERVE

Allow pie to rest for 1 hour prior to serving. You can always refrigerate it once cooled and reheat in a moderate oven later – just ensure to cover with foil.

NOTE

This pastry freezes well – remove from freezer and allow to defrost in the fridge for 3 hours or overnight before rolling. A handy option if you end up with extra pastry.

I still can't believe how easy this is to make!

After the success of the Lazy Breakfast Loaf from *Everyday Thermo Cooking*, I am convinced that my 'prove in a bread tin' approach is the easiest and most efficient way for the home cook to bake bread. Once you've tried it, you'll agree! You literally don't even need to touch the dough, so there's zero technique required, yet the end result has all the hallmarks of a great loaf. This time I've gone with an olive bread, which seems ever so decadent but really is no more difficult than your standard loaf (if you've got a thermo cooker, that is!).

FOOLPROOF OLIVE BREAD

570g warm filtered water
750g baker's flour
2½ teaspoons fine salt
1 teaspoon dried yeast
200g pitted Kalamata olives
Extra flour, if needed

MAKES 1 LOAF

DAIRY FREE
VEGETARIAN
VEGAN

1. Place water, flour, salt and yeast in TC bowl, mix for 6 seconds, speed 6.
2. Add 100g olives, knead for 1 minute, dough function, while slowly adding remaining 100g olives through the hole in the lid.
3. Invert TC bowl over 900g jumbo bread tin and twist the blades, allowing dough to pour into the tin. If you can't move the blades, then the mixture is too wet. Add 2 heaped tablespoons of flour and knead on interval speed for another 10 seconds. Use a silicone spatula to smooth the dough evenly across the bottom of the tin.
4. Cover with a clean tea towel or shower cap and leave for 4–10 hours, or until the dough has risen approx. 2cm from the top of the tin. If you want the dough to rise quickly, place in a warm spot, or if you want it to rise slowly (perhaps overnight) put it in a cool spot.
5. Once dough has risen, preheat oven to 230°C.
6. Place tin in oven and bake for 30 minutes.
7. Using oven mitts, turn tin on its side and shake to release loaf. Continue cooking loaf on oven rack for 10 minutes, or until bread is browned and the crust is hard when knocked.

TO SERVE

Transfer to a wire rack to cool, and try to wait at least 30 minutes before slicing, although it's difficult!

VARIATION

Add a handful of fresh rosemary at step 1.

I just love that this fluffy and moist cake contains half a kilo of vegetables! While I haven't reinvented the wheel when it comes to this classic sweet treat, I have certainly shown how the thermo cooker makes it a whole lot quicker. All those carrots grated in 4 seconds; you'll have the mixture in the oven in no time at all!

CARROT CAKE

500g carrots, quartered
(approx. 4)
250g plain flour
200g brown sugar
160g macadamia oil
2 free-range eggs
2 teaspoons mixed spice
2 teaspoons baking powder
⅓ teaspoon bicarbonate of
soda
¼ teaspoon fine salt

MAKES 1 CAKE

DAIRY FREE
VEGETARIAN

QUICK FIX + BAKING

1. Preheat oven to 175°C. Line the base and sides of a greased 12 x 24cm loaf tin with baking paper.

2. Place carrot in TC bowl, chop for 4 seconds, speed 5.

3. Add flour, sugar, oil, eggs, spice, baking powder, bicarbonate of soda and salt, mix for 20 seconds, reverse speed 3. Scrape down sides.

4. Mix for a further 10 seconds, reverse speed 3, or until mixture is combined and no longer floury. Pour mixture into lined tin and bake for 1 hour or until a skewer inserted comes out clean. Stand for 10 minutes before removing cake from tin and allow to cool completely on a wire rack.

TO SERVE

To serve, ice with maple cream-cheese frosting (page 213).

I love the chunky bits
of fig and apricot.

My mum Janene is famous for this loaf – people just can't get enough of it (especially me!). It's jam-packed with big chunks of decadent figs, apricots, dates and prunes, a far cry from the handful of sultanas you find in commercial loaves. By using 100% rye flour we've not only kept this loaf wheat free, but made it dense and flavoursome, which perfectly suits the rich combination of spices. It was no easy task perfecting this recipe, so I am hugely grateful for Mum's passion and determination, and thrilled we can share it with you.

MUM'S RYE FRUIT BREAD

570g rye flour
1½ teaspoons fine salt
1½ teaspoons cream of tartar
20g brown sugar
2 teaspoons dried yeast
2 teaspoons ground cinnamon
1 teaspoon ground allspice
1 teaspoon ground cloves
1 teaspoon fennel seeds
160g dried figs, cut in half and
	stems removed
100g dates, pitted
100g dried apricots
100g prunes or raisins
60g pumpkin seeds
570g warm water
Poppy seeds, for sprinkling

MAKES 1 LOAF

DAIRY FREE
VEGETARIAN
VEGAN

1. Place flour, salt, cream of tartar, sugar, yeast, cinnamon, allspice, cloves and fennel seeds into TC bowl, mix for 10 seconds, speed 6.

2. Add figs, dates, apricots, prunes or raisins and pumpkin seeds, mix for 5 seconds, reverse speed 4.

3. Add water, knead for 40 seconds, dough function, assisting with spatula.

4. Tip dough into an oiled bowl. Using a silicone spatula, move the dough around until all flour is incorporated.

5. Cover with a tea towel and set aside in a warm place until increased in size by half (approx. 2 hours).

6. Transfer dough into a 680g sandwich bread tin, then use a wet silicone spatula to smooth the top of the dough. Shape the edges of the loaf, pushing down between the dough and the bread tin all the way around. Cover with a tea towel or shower cap and leave to prove in a warm place until dough is 1–2cm from the top of the tin.

7. Preheat oven to 220°C. Spray top of loaf with water and sprinkle with poppy seeds. Place bread in oven and immediately reduce temperature to 200°C. Bake for 40 minutes, then remove bread from tin and continue to bake on oven rack for a further 20 minutes.

TO SERVE
Remove from oven and cool completely on a wire rack before slicing thickly and serving with lashings of butter.

This bread has the most amazing crusty crust and soft fluffy middle – I am so in love! I've been baking these rolls for years and always receive so many compliments, but it was only recently when Ellen was pestering me for the recipe that I realised I had never written it down! Instead I simply rely on ingredient proportions and hydration percentages, so this really is my secret formula. I hope it becomes your go-to formula also!

BASIC BREAD ROLLS

600g baker's flour, plus extra for
   dusting
450g warm water
1½ teaspoons dried yeast
1½ teaspoons fine salt
Oil, for proving bowl

MAKES 8

DAIRY FREE
VEGETARIAN
VEGAN

1. Place flour, water, yeast and salt in TC bowl, mix for 6 seconds, speed 6.

2. Knead for 2 minutes, interval speed. You are looking for a sticky consistency where the dough adheres to the bottom of the bowl but releases from the sides. Add a tablespoon more flour if necessary.

3. Tip dough out into a large oiled bowl. Cover with a tea towel or shower cap and set aside in a warm place for 2 hours or until doubled in size.

4. Turn dough out onto a lightly floured surface and divide into 8 roughly even pieces. Shape each piece into a ball, creating tension and keeping them as tight as possible. Place rolls on a baking tray lined with baking paper, leaving 2cm between each. Cover with a tea towel and set aside in a warm place for 30 minutes.

5. Meanwhile, preheat oven to 230°C.

6. Spray rolls with water, then place in oven and bake for 15–20 minutes, or until rolls are browned top and bottom.

TO SERVE

Allow to cool on a wire rack for a minimum of 15 minutes before serving. Once completely cooled, store in a bread bag at room temperature.

This is a brilliant alternative to the classic sugar icing – it still gives that glossy finish without being sickly sweet. I call it my friendly frosting as it suits almost all eating preferences, and who doesn't love a slice of cake?

FRIENDLY FROSTING

150g white sugar
400g coconut cream
2 teaspoons xanthan gum (see note)

MAKES 2 CUPS

DAIRY FREE
GLUTEN FREE
VEGETARIAN
VEGAN

QUICK FIX

1. Place sugar in TC bowl, mill for 20 seconds, speed 10. Scrape down sides.

2. Add coconut cream and xanthan gum, mix for 30 seconds, speed 4. Pour icing immediately onto cake and work quickly to spread evenly.

TO SERVE

Refrigerate frosted cake for a minimum 30 minutes before serving. Once frosting has set it doesn't need to be kept in the fridge, but the consistency is better when it's cool.

NOTE

Xanthan gum is found in the baking aisle of some supermarkets and health food stores, and can also be ordered online. It's a natural thickener and stabiliser used in many health foods and beauty products. I use it in my homemade make-up remover, as well as my friendly frosting.

VARIATION

The quantity of sugar isn't essential for this recipe – you can increase or decrease the amounts based on personal preference. For a sugar-free alternative, replace sugar with xylitol.

See page 198 for picture!

My go-to icing, because it's just so easy! And of course, so delicious . . . you'll find me licking it off the spatula! By using maple syrup we are attaining a beautiful caramel sweetness without any refined sugar. And because we've kept the flavour mellow, this icing pairs really well with almost any baked good – my favourite would be the carrot cake on page 207.

MAPLE CREAM CHEESE FROSTING

250g cream cheese, roughly chopped
70g maple syrup

MAKES 1 CUP

GLUTEN FREE
VEGETARIAN

QUICK FIX

1. Insert butterfly into TC bowl. Add cream cheese and maple syrup, whip for 1 minute, speed 4.

TO SERVE
Use immediately or refrigerate for up to 3 days.

VARIATION
Add 1 teaspoon vanilla bean paste or vanilla extract, or a couple of drops of food grade orange oil.

NOTE
Ensure cake has completely cooled before icing.

We used it in the carrot cake, page 206.

My other sister Loryn is behind the
camera taking all of the photos,
and making Mum and I laugh!

winter warmers

I am very much a breakfast person, especially in the cooler months. So here's my collection of warming winter breakfasts, to make it just that little bit easier to get out of bed on cold mornings. In my typical fashion, there's a selection of recipes that can be whipped up mid-week and ready in under 15 minutes, and a few favourites more suited to leisurely weekend mornings. While I've loosely classified these as breakfast recipes, that's really selling them short — some could also be lunch, some could be dessert, and some could be for in-between.

Baked apple
is the perfect
winter topping.

This is one of my favourite breakfasts – oats loaded with all the good stuff! This is my 'breakfast of champions'. Not only will the oats keep you full and satisfied, but the nuts and seeds add a dose of protein and fibre to really seal the deal. Like many of my breakfasts, I've stuck to pantry-staple ingredients to keep life simple. However, if you've got fresh fruit on hand, by all means add it in at the 'flavouring' section.

LOADED OATS

50g raw nuts – macadamia,
    cashew, almond
2 tablespoons flaxseeds
600g water
100g rolled oats (not instant)
Pinch salt
3 tablespoons chia seeds
40g sweetener, or to taste –
    honey, maple syrup, agave
    syrup, brown sugar
Flavouring – ½ teaspoon vanilla
    bean paste, ½ teaspoon
    ground cinnamon, 50g
    sultanas, 1 grated apple,
    1 thinly sliced banana or
    1 cup blueberries

1. Place nuts and flaxseeds in TC bowl, mill for 20 seconds, speed 10. Remove from the TC bowl and set aside.

2. Without cleaning bowl add water, oats and salt, cook for 12 minutes, 90°C, reverse speed soft.

3. Add reserved nut mixture, chia seeds, sweetener and flavouring, mix for 10 seconds, reverse speed 3. Allow to stand in TC bowl for 5 minutes before serving.

TO SERVE

Serve topped with fresh fruit, cream, yoghurt, milk, dried fruit, or extra nuts and seeds.

SERVES 3

DAIRY FREE
VEGETARIAN
VEGAN (OPTION)

QUICK FIX

Goats cheese is my favourite topping!

Like your classic tin of baked beans, only much, much better! And it takes only 15 minutes to put together. While this recipe certainly fits the breakfast mould, it also makes a cracking quick dinner, especially with a fried egg on top. At a pinch you could even up the smoky paprika and serve these with corn chips – nachos, anyone?

BREAKFAST BEANS

1 brown onion, peeled and halved

2 garlic cloves, peeled

1 long red chilli

20g olive oil

400g canned tomatoes

80g tomato paste

40g Worcestershire sauce

2 teaspoons Dijon mustard

1 teaspoon dried basil or fresh thyme leaves

½ teaspoon smoked paprika

½ teaspoon fine salt

800g canned four bean mix, rinsed and drained

SERVES 4

DAIRY FREE
GLUTEN FREE
VEGETARIAN (OPTION)
VEGAN (OPTION)

QUICK FIX

1. Place onion, garlic and chilli in TC bowl, chop 5 seconds, speed 5. Scrape down sides.

2. Add oil, sauté 5 minutes, 100°C, speed 1.

3. Add tomatoes, tomato paste, Worcestershire sauce, mustard, herbs, paprika and salt, cook for 4 minutes, 100°C, speed 1.

4. Add beans, warm for 2 minutes, 100°C, reverse speed soft.

TO SERVE

Serve with toast, eggs, cheese, sautéed mushrooms, wilted spinach or corn chips.

VARIATION

Any canned beans can be used for this recipe – cannellini beans are a favourite. We usually use a mild long red chilli, but for a fiery option try a bird's eye!

NOTE

Ensure Worcestershire sauce does not contain anchovies for a vegetarian and vegan dish.

I love the combo of maple syrup, bananas and roasted almonds.

Pancakes were the very first thing I ever learnt to cook as a child and were a weekend favourite. Although back then my recipe was a little more basic – a mug of flour, a mug of milk, an egg. While I adore the simplicity of my original formula, these pancakes are much, much fluffier and definitely more delicious! In fact, they're so good that most of the time we don't even bother with the toppings.

FLUFFY PANCAKES

50g butter, plus extra for
  greasing pan
30g raw sugar
600g buttermilk
2 free-range eggs
260g plain flour
2 teaspoons baking powder
1 teaspoon bicarbonate of soda
¼ teaspoon fine salt

SERVES 4

VEGETARIAN

QUICK FIX

1. Place butter and sugar in TC bowl, melt for 3 minutes, 60°C speed 2.
2. Add buttermilk and eggs, mix for 4 seconds, speed 4.
3. Add flour, baking powder, bicarbonate of soda and salt, mix for 5 seconds, speed 3. Scrape down sides.
4. Mix for a further 5 seconds, speed 3. The batter should still have small lumps. Refrigerate batter for up to 12 hours, or begin cooking immediately.
5. Heat fry pan on medium heat. Swirl ½ teaspoon butter to grease pan.
6. Using a ladle or cup, spoon ½ cup pancake batter into pan. When pancake forms bubbles on top, flip over and cook until golden on the bottom (approx. 4 minutes in total).
7. Repeat with remaining batter, keeping cooked pancakes in oven covered with foil or in a food warmer.

TO SERVE

Top pancakes with slices of fresh or cooked fruit, nuts, seeds, youghurt, cream, honey or maple syrup.

VARIATION

You can add 1 cup fresh blueberries at step 4. Fold in with spatula after mixing in the flour.

*Cooking is love
made visible.*

I love how rich and creamy this dairy-free drink is.

Very much a family affair, followers of our social media will know that it's my younger sister Ellen who develops many of our vegan recipes, including this one! Her clever swaps make this delicious drink dairy free and a nourishing breakfast or afternoon sweet treat. This is one of my favourites during the winter months – I love the fact that it takes less than 10 minutes to whip up and all the ingredients are pantry staples. And it doesn't taste healthy!

ELLEN'S HOT CHOCCY

60g raw cashews
550g water
15g cocoa powder
10g brown sugar (or sweetener of choice)
4 medjool dates, pitted
Pinch salt

SERVES 2

DAIRY FREE
GLUTEN FREE
VEGETARIAN
VEGAN

QUICK FIX

1. Put all ingredients in TC bowl, heat 7 minutes, 90°C, speed 2.
2. Blend 1 minute, speed 9.

TO SERVE

Serve immediately and enjoy.

NOTE

The nuts and dates give this drink a rich thickness, but also mean it doesn't keep well – best enjoyed freshly made.

VARIATION

For a more substantial breakfast option, add protein powder.

I love the breakfast crumble – it's basically a fancy way to serve stewed fruit and granola, yet it's so easy to pull together and serve. In summer you could substitute the apple and rhubarb with plums, peaches or apricots, or perhaps throw in some blueberries and raspberries. Of course, it could also double as a dessert, in which case you might want to up the coconut sugar in the crumble topping.

APPLE RHUBARB BREAKFAST CRUMBLE

½ orange, rind and juice

25g raw sugar

500g trimmed rhubarb, cut into 2cm pieces

500g Granny Smith apples, peeled, cored and roughly chopped

100g raw almonds

100g rolled oats

100g solid coconut oil (see note)

50g wholemeal spelt flour

50g pumpkin seeds

30g chia seeds

50g coconut sugar or to taste

1 teaspoon ground cinnamon

Pinch salt

SERVES 6

DAIRY FREE
VEGETARIAN
VEGAN

1. Preheat oven to 180°C.

2. Place orange rind and raw sugar in TC bowl, mill for 10 seconds, speed 8.

3. Transfer to a medium casserole dish and toss with rhubarb, apple and orange juice. Cover and bake for 30 minutes, or until just tender.

4. Meanwhile, place almonds in a clean TC bowl, mill for 3 seconds, speed 5.

5. Add oats, coconut oil, flour, pumpkin seeds, chia seeds, coconut sugar, cinnamon and salt, mix for 5 seconds, reverse speed 3.

6. Once fruit has cooked, top with crumble mixture. Bake, uncovered, for 15 minutes, or until crumble is golden.

TO SERVE

Delicious warm or cold. You can top with cream, yoghurt, coconut yoghurt or custard, but it's perfect served just as it is.

NOTE

Coconut oil will be solid at cooler temperatures and liquid when it's warmer. If necessary, pop your jar in the fridge or freezer for 15 minutes to solidify the oil before making this recipe.

This recipe is such a great way to cook pears – you've got the beautiful quarters that hold their shape perfectly in the steaming tray along with a deliciously sweet syrup that forms in the thermo bowl from the steaming liquid. While I love these with yoghurt and granola for breakfast, I think they might be best served with a big scoop of homemade butterscotch ice-cream for dessert (my super easy recipe can be found in *Everyday Thermo Cooking!*).

VANILLA POACHED PEARS

150g water

100g brown sugar

1 cinnamon stick

1 vanilla bean, halved and split
    down the middle

4 Bosc pears, peeled, quartered
    and cored

1 lemon, juice only

SERVES 4

DAIRY FREE

GLUTEN FREE

VEGETARIAN

VEGAN

QUICK FIX

1. Place water, sugar, cinnamon and vanilla bean in TC bowl. Toss pears in lemon juice and place in lower steaming tray. Steam for 20 minutes, steaming temperature, reverse speed 2.

TO SERVE

Transfer pears to serving bowl and pour over vanilla syrup from TC bowl. Serve warm or refrigerate for later. Delicious with cream, yoghurt, mascarpone, coconut yoghurt, granola, muesli or even fluffy pancakes (page 221).

NOTE

Check pears are cooked through after step 1, and if not, continue to steam any uncooked pears for a further 3 minutes, steaming temperature, reverse speed 2. If liquid in TC bowl isn't syrupy, continue cooking for 10 minutes, steaming temperature, reverse speed 1 until reduced.

A NEW WAY TO ENTERTAIN

I used to be one for lavish dinners at restaurants, but now my absolute favourite celebrations are at home, where the only noisy patrons are us! There's no time limits on the table or closing times, no loud music, everyone can shuffle around and pets are invited. It's relaxed, fun and intimate, no matter the group size – there's always a sense of festivity when too many chairs are squashed around the table. And of course, everything tastes better when it's homemade with love! Not to mention all the money you'll save. But I know what you're thinking – so much work!

Introducing my version of entertaining – the 'pot luck dinner'. Every single attendee must cook a dish to share with the group, either a starter, main or dessert. It must be a secret, and it mustn't be something they've cooked for a previous pot luck. Bring it along, load everything onto the middle of the table, sit down and enjoy. Easy as that! Listen with intrigue as everyone proudly explains what they've made, and laugh as you see how many desserts you've ended up with.

Everyone does a little bit, and no one does a lot. I promise you'll be entertaining a lot more! I also love the fact that it forces everyone to get involved and try their hand at a dish, even if they're not the most confident cook (particularly the men!). The number of times I've heard someone say 'But I can't cook!' and then turn up with a masterpiece – I think they just needed the push to give it a go. And you know what, even if a dish is a complete fail, it's no stress as there's so much other delicious food!

My family does weekly pot luck dinners, and I don't think you'd find more love and laughs in one room. My girlfriends and I do a monthly pot luck, rotating around each of our houses to host, where we chuckle into the early hours. We even do pot lucks for our staff social get-togethers!

Entertaining is meant to be fun and energising – a place to connect with friends and loved ones, a place to reminisce and laugh about old memories, a space to acknowledge and celebrate milestones and achievements. It's about so much more than a perfect menu! It's not a time for anyone to be chained to the kitchen, stressed and missing out on their guests' company – when I host I'm always sitting at the table laughing along with everyone else.

So instead of giving you another entertaining menu, here I've given you a new way to entertain.

My advice for pot luck dish selection: avoid anything that must be served immediately once cooked – deep frying is out! Instead, choose dishes that improve with age (ragus and curry), dishes that need to cool or are served cold (baked goods and dips), or dishes that simply require assembly (grazing platters and salads). A food warmer with a lockable lid is a handy accessory for transporting and serving anything hot.

My pot luck picks:

- **Harissa eggplant dip** (page 85) with crackers and vegetable crudités
- **Foolproof olive bread** (page 205)
- **Simple summer tart**s (page 83)
- **Veggie gyoza** (page 159) with **Peanut dipping sauce** (page 49)
- **Spring salad with miso dressing** (page 27)
- **Potato gnocchi** (page 171) with **Vegetable bolognaise** (page 151)
- **Apple pie with flaky pastry** (page 201)

WHAT'S IN THE FRIDGE?

For me, there are so many nights when I get home with no idea what I'll cook – I simply open the fridge, see what ingredients I've got on hand and make something up from there. Very rarely do I follow a particular recipe; instead I'm looking for creative ways to incorporate seasonal produce, use up leftovers and avoid waste. Having said all this, I certainly have my basic recipe ideas that I simply slot different ingredients into – a quiche, creamy pasta, risotto, pizza, soup or salad. I call these my recipe 'guides', and it's these that I share in this final chapter. These guides supersede seasons and geographic location, can be tailored to any family's tastes or eating preferences, and will save you time and money. They will also have you wasting less food – a win for you, the environment, and all those who go without, as I believe when you honour what you have, you honour what others don't. Forget fancy recipes, here I'm focusing on the realities of life – you're not always going to have the exact ingredients, but you can still whip up something delicious and nutritious with the pieces you have on hand. You'll be looking at that leftover roast pumpkin or half a head of broccoli in a whole new light!

This is such an easy recipe to cook, and the result is really quite impressive! I use a fry pan to create the tart shell, so there's no need to go out and invest (and store!) fancy equipment. You'll have the whole thing finished and on the table in less than 30 minutes, and any leftovers are delicious cold in lunchboxes.

ROUGH PUFF TART

2 sheets butter puff pastry

3 cups ready-to-eat vegetables – grilled zucchini, roasted pumpkin, grilled eggplant, roasted potatoes, tomatoes, spinach, grilled asparagus, roasted onion, kale, spring onions, grated carrot, sautéed mushrooms, steamed broccoli

400g can beans, drained (optional) – chickpeas, kidney beans, 4 bean mix

100g cheese, roughly chopped (optional) – parmesan, cheddar, tasty, feta

8 free-range eggs

100g cream (any type is fine)

2 teaspoons salt – flavour bomb paste (see page 63), mushroom salt or fine salt

Garnishes – crumbled or grated cheese, parsley, dill, sprouts, pine nuts, chilli flakes

SERVES 6

VEGETARIAN

QUICK FIX

1. Preheat oven to 200°C. Line a 26cm ovenproof fry pan with a single piece of baking paper ensuring a 10cm overhang.

2. Place one pastry sheet in the bottom of the lined pan. Cut the second sheet into 4 long strips and use these to line the sides of the fry pan. It's fine for the pastry to overhang the sides of the pan. Press the pastry together to seal. Fill the pastry with vegetables and beans (if using).

3. Place cheese in TC bowl (if using), grate for 5 seconds, speed 8.

4. Add eggs, cream and salt, mix for 10 seconds, speed 4. Pour over vegetables and beans.

5. Transfer to oven and bake for 20 minutes, or until egg mixture is set and pastry edges are golden. Lift tart from fry pan using the baking paper and transfer to a serving board.

TO SERVE

Serve hot or cold with garnishes, a side salad and chutney or relish.

*Just add whatever veggies
you have on hand!*

This recipe is an absolute gem – no matter where I am I can almost always find enough ingredients to whip up this meal! It's also an easy one to adapt to any crowd size: double ingredients for eight, or quarter for one. Just make sure the sauce reaches 100°C in step 4.

EASY CREAMY PASTA

400g pasta – spaghetti, penne, buckwheat pasta, gluten-free pasta
4 garlic cloves, peeled
50g olive oil
150g creamy ingredient – cream, mascarpone, olive oil, pesto
4–6 cups ready-to-eat veggies – baby spinach, rocket, roasted pumpkin, roasted mushrooms, tomatoes, grilled asparagus, steamed broccoli, steamed green beans, cooked peas, zucchini, corn kernels, roasted onion, olives, capsicum

SERVES 4

DAIRY FREE (OPTION)
GLUTEN FREE (OPTION)
VEGETARIAN
VEGAN (OPTION)

QUICK FIX

Salt, to taste – stock concentrate (see page 249), smoked salt, fine salt, mushroom salt, flavour bomb paste (see page 63)
Toppings, to serve – basil, parsley, toasted pine nuts, toasted almonds, cheese, chilli flakes, spring onion, sesame seeds, dukkah (see page 35)

1. Cook pasta on stove according to packet instructions. Drain and reserve 50g of the starchy pasta cooking water.
2. Meanwhile, place garlic in TC bowl, chop for 3 seconds, speed 6. Scrape down sides.
3. Add oil, sauté for 5 minutes, 100°C, speed 1.
4. Add creamy ingredient, salt and reserved pasta water, heat for 2 minutes, 100°C, speed 2.
5. Toss cooked pasta, cream sauce and ready-to-eat veggies together in a very large bowl.

TO SERVE
Sprinkle with toppings and serve. Delicious served immediately or packed in lunchboxes cold.

NOTE
If your veggies are coming straight from the fridge you might want to heat them up on the stove before tossing with other ingredients. However, if the veggies are still warm from cooking or are at room temperature then there's no need to dirty extra dishes by reheating.

This soup sounds too healthy to be delicious, but it's surprisingly tasty and satisfying! It's such an easy way to use up bits and pieces of fresh produce left in the fridge, especially because nothing needs to be precooked. Ellen came up with this fuss-free gem, and it's one I've happily added to my quick dinner repertoire.

NOURISHING QUINOA VEGGIE SOUP

1 onion, peeled and halved – white onion, brown onion, shallot, leek

20g oil – macadamia, olive, grapeseed

400g heavy vegetables, cut into bite-size pieces – carrot, potato, sweet potato, broccoli, celery, capsicum, cauliflower

850g water

60g stock concentrate (see page 249)

Herbs and spices, to taste – chilli flakes, fresh thyme leaves, dried basil, dried oregano, dried coriander, ground cumin seeds, ground turmeric

200g light vegetables, cut into bite-size pieces – corn kernels, peas, zucchini, kale, spinach, silver beet, broccolini, snow peas, beans

80g quinoa – any type

SERVES 4

DAIRY FREE
GLUTEN FREE
VEGETARIAN
VEGAN

QUICK FIX

1. Place onion in TC bowl, chop for 5 seconds, speed 5. Scrape down sides.
2. Add oil, sauté for 5 minutes, 100°C, speed 1.
3. Add heavy vegetables, water, stock concentrate, herbs and spices, cook for 10 minutes, 100°C, reverse speed 1.
4. Add light vegetables and quinoa, cook for 8 minutes, 100°C, reverse speed 2, or until vegetables and quinoa are cooked. Taste and add salt or additional herbs and spices as required.

TO SERVE

Serve immediately, refrigerate for up to 5 days or freeze. Garnish with fresh herbs, additional spices, pine nuts or grated cheese.

Simple yet tasty, this easy meal requires only fresh veggies and pantry staples. And if you're really in a pinch, you can replace the fresh veggies with frozen ones!

RICE + VEGGIE BAKE

1.3 litres water

400g medium grain rice

2 brown onions, peeled and halved

2 garlic cloves, peeled

40g olive oil

200 raw cashews

40g stock concentrate (see page 249)

40g Dijon mustard

5 tablespoons nutritional yeast flakes

1 teaspoon fine salt

300g vegetables, diced – carrot, zucchini, peas, corn, cauliflower, broccoli, capsicum, spring onions

400g can beans, rinsed – chickpeas, kidney beans

SERVES 5

DAIRY FREE
GLUTEN FREE
VEGETARIAN
VEGAN

QUICK FIX

1. Preheat oven to 180°C.
2. Fill TC bowl with 1 litre of water. Place rice in steamer basket and rinse for 10 seconds, speed 5.
3. Steam for 20 minutes, steaming temperature, speed 3, or until cooked. Spread out evenly in a large casserole dish.
4. Place onion and garlic in clean TC bowl, chop for 5 seconds, speed 5. Scrape down sides.
5. Add olive oil, sauté for 5 minutes, 100°C, speed 1.
6. Add 300g water, cashews, stock concentrate, Dijon mustard, nutritional yeast flakes and salt. Blend for 40 seconds, speed 9, or until smooth.
7. Add vegetables and beans, combine using a spatula. Pour mixture evenly over rice.
8. Bake for 20 minutes, or until top is slightly golden and vegetables are cooked through.

TO SERVE

Enjoy hot immediately or cold the next day. Can be reheated in a moderate oven.

VARIATION

Sprinkle with spring onions or grated cheese before baking.

I promise making your own pizza base is easy! The thermo does all the technical stuff for you – the only trick is getting organised and whipping up the dough a couple of hours before dinner (or my preferred option, the night before). This is one of the best ways to use up lots of little titbits in the fridge – every pizza can have a different sauce, cheese and toppings!

PIZZA PIZZA

220g water
1 tablespoon dried yeast
500g plain flour
60g olive oil
2 teaspoons fine salt
2 teaspoons sugar
250g sauce – tomato passata
(page 129), tomato paste,
pesto, harissa eggplant dip
(page 85), babaganoush
150g cheese – grated
mozzarella, crumbled feta,
shaved parmesan, grated
cheddar
2 cups toppings – tomatoes,
steamed broccoli, sautéed
mushrooms, roasted
pumpkin, sundried
tomatoes, olives,
marinated artichokes, basil,
thyme, baby spinach,
roasted capsicum, roasted
eggplant, chilli, cooked
potato, zucchini, onion

SERVES 4

VEGETARIAN

Garnishes (optional) – rocket,
sprouts, micro herbs, chilli
flakes, extra cheese, pine
nuts, chilli oil (see page 37),
garlic crumbs (see page 41),
chilli chutney (see page 139)

1. Place water, yeast, flour, oil, salt and sugar in TC bowl, mix for 6 seconds, speed 6.

2. Set dial to closed lid position, knead for 2 minutes, interval speed. Tip dough out onto a clean bench and shape into a ball. Place dough in an oiled bowl, cover and stand in a warm place for 1 hour, or until the dough has doubled in size. Alternatively, refrigerate dough for 12–24 hours.

3. Preheat oven and 2 baking trays or pizza stones to 220°C.

4. Divide dough into 4 equal portions and roll out thinly on baking mats or baking paper. If your oven is small you may want to roll into ovals so you can easily fit 2 to an oven tray.

5. Spread each with sauce, toppings and cheese, leaving a 1cm border around the edges. Place on hot oven trays and bake for 15 minutes or until crust is golden and cheese has melted.

TO SERVE

Serve immediately topped with garnishes and a drizzle of olive oil. We like a dab of chilli chutney on the crusts.

Not only do I prefer brown rice in risottos because it is less processed than its white counterpart, it also brings so much more flavour! It gives a nutty richness, making this risotto a hearty and satisfying meal. I love how easy my thermo cooker makes this dish – while it does need nearly an hour cooking, almost all of that time is hands-off.

'THE' BROWN RICE RISOTTO

1 onion, peeled and halved – leek, brown onion, shallot, white onion
2 garlic cloves, peeled
40g olive oil
300g brown rice
1kg chicken stock, vegetable stock or 940g water and 60g stock concentrate
100g white wine or additional stock
2 cups ready to eat vegetables – spinach, chopped tomatoes, roasted pumpkin, roasted cauliflower, sautéed mush-rooms, thawed frozen peas or corn, steamed asparagus, steamed beetroot, steamed broccoli, grated zucchini

40g dairy (optional) – butter, mascarpone, grated cheese, cream
Toppings – feta cheese, ricotta cheese, burrata, mint, basil, parsley, toasted pine nuts, olives, pesto, rocket

1. Place onion and garlic in TC bowl, chop for 5 seconds, speed 5. Scrape down sides.
2. Add olive oil, sauté for 5 minutes, 100°C, speed 1.
3. Add rice, sauté for 2 minutes, 100°C, speed 1.
4. Add stock and wine, cook for 50 minutes, 100°C, reverse speed 1.5.
5. Add vegetables and dairy (if using), combine using a spatula. Cook for 3 minutes, 100°C, reverse speed 1.5. Allow to stand in TC bowl for 5 minutes before serving.

TO SERVE
Divide between 4 serving bowls and add toppings.

SERVES 4

DAIRY FREE (OPTION)
GLUTEN FREE
VEGETARIAN
VEGAN (OPTION)

This delicious pho broth is my sister Loryn's magic formula, and as the name suggests it is absolutely full of flavour! You'd be fooled into thinking it had been simmering on the stove for hours. While the ingredient list is longer than I usually like, you'll have most, if not all of it in the pantry already, and the method is super short (so I figure it balances out!).

LORYN'S FLAVOURFUL PHO

1 brown onion, peeled and halved
1 long red chilli
3 garlic cloves, peeled
3cm piece ginger, peeled
20g toasted sesame oil
8 cloves
4 star anise
2 cinnamon sticks
1 teaspoon ground coriander seeds
½ teaspoon fennel seeds

120g tamari
60g miso paste (see note)
20g maple syrup
2 shiitake mushrooms (fresh or dried)
40g stock concentrate (see page 249)
1.7 litres water
Cooked noodles – flat rice noodles, udon noodles, soba noodles, kelp noodles

4 cups ready-to-eat vegetables – snow peas, bok choy, spinach, choy sum, spring onions, grated carrot, grated zucchini, steamed broccoli, steamed broccolini, sauteed mushrooms
Toppings – fried shallots, bean sprouts, lime wedges, coriander, mint, Thai basil, chilli, sriracha

SERVES 4

DAIRY FREE
GLUTEN FREE (OPTION)
VEGETARIAN
VEGAN

1. Place onion, chilli, garlic and ginger in TC bowl, chop for 5 seconds, speed 5. Scrape down sides.

2. Add oil, cloves, star anise, cinnamon, coriander and fennel seeds, sauté for 6 minutes, 100°C, speed 1.

3. Add tamari, miso paste, maple syrup, shiitake mushrooms, stock concentrate and water, cook for 30 minutes, 100°C, speed 1.5. Strain through a fine sieve.

TO SERVE

Divide noodles and vegetables between 4 serving bowls, pour over broth and garnish with toppings. Leftover broth can be frozen in plastic containers and defrosted for later meals.

NOTE

I like to use red miso paste for this recipe but whatever you have on hand is fine.

Stock concentrate is a staple in most savoury thermo cooker recipes, and for good reason, as the salt lifts all the flavours in the dish and the herbs and vegetables add extra seasoning. Use it wherever you would usually use salt, a stock cube or liquid stock. Add a tablespoon to ragus, pasta sauces, soups, risottos, gravies, curries or stews. But you don't need a recipe! And you certainly don't need to shop for the ingredients. This is the ultimate 'clean out the veggie draw' guide – simply use whatever odds and ends are available in your fridge. Think of the times you've bought a bunch of spring onions and only used a couple, a bunch of herbs and only used a few sprigs, or a kilo of pumpkin but only needed 800 grams. Or when you've bought a punnet of tomatoes for a salad, but never got around to making it; the tomatoes might not be looking their freshest, but they will do perfectly well blended and cooked into a stock concentrate.

STOCK CONCENTRATE

600g vegetables, roughly chopped – carrots, celery, pumpkin, zucchini, capsicum, sweet potato, rocket, spinach, lettuce, spring onions, tomatoes, cabbage, broccoli (stalks), asparagus (woody ends)
1 onion, peeled and halved
2 garlic cloves, peeled
2 handfuls fresh herbs
150g rock salt
50g olive oil

MAKES 1L

DAIRY FREE
GLUTEN FREE
VEGETARIAN
VEGAN

QUICK FIX

1. Place vegetables, onion, garlic and herbs in TC bowl, chop for 6 seconds, speed 7, assisting with spatula. Scrape down sides.
2. Add salt and oil, cook for 20 minutes, 100°C, speed 2.
3. Purée for 1 minute, speed 9.

STORAGE

Allow to cool before transferring to sterilised glass jars and storing in the fridge for up to 3 months.

NOTE

You can freeze stock concentrate in ice cube trays and simply pop out a cube on demand for an approximate tablespoon. This is an especially useful option if you are very slow to use it up.

WASTE NOT WANT NOT

Other than water, there may not be a more precious commodity than food – yet still we waste so much of it! But I'm on a mission to change that, by providing you with the tools to think differently and get creative with your cooking. The recipe guides in this chapter are my first line of attack, and below I've listed some commonly wasted ingredients and show you how you can turn them from trash into treasure!

- **Bread** – Turn stale bread into breadcrumbs or croutons. These add texture and flavour to salads, bakes, roast veggies, pasta dishes . . . anything savoury, really! Try my Garlic crumbs (see page 41), or simply toss cubed bread in oil and bake for 15 minutes at 175°C.

- **Herbs** – Fill ice cube trays with finely chopped fresh herbs, then top up with white wine, stock or olive oil. Freeze, then use to add fresh flavour to savoury dishes – pop a cube in your pasta sauce or use to deglaze your pan. Alternatively, make a batch of Stock Concentrate (see page 249) – it's probably the most versatile flavour maker to have on hand!

- **Milk** – Make yoghurt! It will extend the life of your milk, plus make it more versatile. My super thick recipe can be found on page 59. Alternatively, blend up milk, frozen fruit and a sweetener for 1 minute, speed 9 for a quick and easy breakfast, afternoon snack or even dessert. Of course, there's always ice-cream, which will land your milk safely in the freezer for enjoyment over the coming months.

- **Pesto and Sauces** – Toss through pasta, add to meatballs, omelettes and frittatas or stir through my Super thick yoghurt (see page 59) or Aioli (see page 45) for a zesty new dipping sauce! I also add spoonfuls of chutneys, jams and relishes to rich, slow-cooked dishes such as ragus and curry for a little sweetness and extra flavour hit.

- **Eggs** – Given their long shelf life it would be unusual to have whole eggs going to waste, but so often we end up with leftover yolks or whites. In this book I've purposely avoided splitting eggs in any of the recipes for this exact reason, but should you end up with egg whites, the obvious answer is to make a pavlova! Or, much simpler, add egg whites to smoothies for an added protein boost (like my Peanut butter banana thickshake, see page 109). With egg yolks I would make a deliciously rich custard, ice-cream or mayonnaise, or I'd toss the yolks through steaming hot spaghetti then add some grated cheese, rocket, olive oil and salt for a satisfying 10-minute meal. I also add any leftover eggy bits to omelettes and scrambled eggs – sometimes they end up a little richer from some extra yolks, sometimes a little lighter and fluffier from the extra whites.

- **Cooked Rice and Pasta** – Add plain to chunky soups like minestrone or laksa, or toss in a generous amount of oil and add to salads. My favourite use for leftover starches is as the filling for omelettes – if using rice, go for an Asian-inspired omelette, adding fresh coriander and a dash of sriracha chilli sauce. For pasta, go with Mediterranean ingredients such as tomatoes, basil and feta, and if you've also got extra pasta sauce, add that in too – give it a go with any leftover Spaghetti bolognaise (see page 175).

- **Meat** – Finely chop and add to salads, soups, rice and pasta dishes like my One bowl tomato spaghetti (see page 23), Rainbow rice (see page 29) and Nourishing quinoa veggie soup (page 239). Providing it's already cooked, simply toss into the recipe at the last step. Use extra coconut milk to thin out that leftover container of curry and turn into a delicious laksa, thin out meat ragus (like my Mexican brisket, see page 155) with extra Tomato passata (see page 129) and use as you would a bolognaise sauce. Don't underestimate how a little meat can go a long way in bringing extra flavour to a dish – no matter how small the leftover, add it as a 'meat seasoning' or garnish. And always keep your bones for making stocks as these are both incredibly flavourful and also choc-full of nutrients (freeze the bones until you're ready and have enough).

- **Veggies** – Most veggies can be pickled in a vinegar solution, extending their shelf life (and often ramping up their flavour!) similar to my 'Canned' Beetroot recipe (see page 141). Fill a large, sterilised glass jar with sliced veggies such as cucumber, carrot, radish, onion, garlic, chilli, fennel, zucchini, celery and capsicum. Then combine equal parts white vinegar and water along with 1 teaspoon of salt and 1 teaspoon of sugar (per 500ml total liquid) and fill the jar, ensuring all veggies are submerged. Store in the fridge for up to 3 months and pull out pickled veggies to add to savoury dishes as you please. Then you can reuse the pickling vinegar! Pauline's piccalilli (see page 137) is a similar technique and is great for heartier produce like cauliflower. Soups are another way to use up veggies that are looking a little sad, as once they're puréed no one will know! You can substitute the cauliflower and carrot in my Creamy cauliflower soup (see page 183) for any combination of cauliflower, carrot, sweet potato and pumpkin; you can add any leafy greens to my Thai zucchini soup (see page 13) – you can even replace some or all of the zucchini with broccoli; and if you've got carrots starting to look shabby, it's a no-brainer – Carrot cake (see page 207)!

- **Fruit** – Smoothies are my number one way to use up fruit that's looking past its prime – once it's blended no one will know! Place something solid (frozen fruit or ice cubes) in the TC bowl along with bits and pieces of fresh fruit (and even veggies!) plus a splash of liquid – this can be a more filling option using milk, coconut milk, or thin yoghurt, or a lighter take using fruit juice, green tea or even water. Blend for 10 seconds, speed 9. Then continue blending for a further 2 minutes, speed 9, while slowly pouring additional liquid through the hole in the TC lid. Done! Apples are a super easy fruit to use up – quarter and grate in the TC bowl for 3 seconds, speed 4. Add grated apple to salads and fresh noodle dishes or stir through porridge, yoghurt or chia puddings. Of course, you could always make an Apple pie with flaky pastry (see page 201) or Spiced apple cake (see page 199). Bananas are also incredibly versatile – once they're nice and ripe use to whip up a batch of Easy ice-cream (see page 93) or a Peanut butter banana thickshake (see page 109). If they've turned black they're perfect for Banana bread (see page 87).

My Larder Love chapter (see page 127) is a great collection of preserving recipes to make fresh produce last months rather than weeks, another handy arsenal in the war on waste. Additionally, check out my Cauliflower pizza bases (see page 17), Fruit jellies (see page 81), Simple summer tarts (see page 83) and Loaded oats (see page 217) – because each of these recipes is written in my 'guide' format enabling you to use what you like, and what you have on hand!

If all else fails, the freezer is always the final frontier. Get your fresh produce frozen and use at a later (more convenient) date. As a general rule, fruit and meat are best frozen raw, while veggies are best frozen par-cooked. For my guide to frozen meals, see Fresh to Freezer (page 87). Don't forget dairy, eggs, bread, baked goods, slices, sauces, pesto, nuts and seeds can also be sent to the freezer!

For more of my Waste Not Want Not recipes, see pages 158–92 in my previous cookbook *Everyday Thermo Cooking*.

ACKNOWLEDGEMENTS

While I may be the face of this cookbook (literally and figuratively!), I am a mere cog in the wheel of brilliantly talented people who have contributed to making this work all that it is. I couldn't be prouder of what we've created. To each of you below – and to so many more – I am bursting with love and gratitude, thank you.

Firstly, thank you to my absolutely amazing family. Your love and support are the anchor and root system that enables me to take flight.

Loryn – as is the case in everything we do, you deserve every accolade for this book, for it is your talent that breathes life into my words and my recipes, and your partnership that empowers me to share myself with the world. You have perfectly embodied my 'fresh' vision in a way only you could, for there is no one who understands me better. Your genius never ceases to awe me, and your big heart never ceases to fill me with gratitude. While I'm doing life with you I'm happy.

Ellen, not only was it a pleasure having you working so closely on this project, it was an absolute necessity. Our frequent impromptu 'vision' chats helped me more than you'd know. You came into your own during this book, and these pages and our readers are far richer for your contribution.

Mum, as with every cookbook, I cannot thank you enough for your behind-the-scenes contribution. The persistence you show for perfecting recipes is inspiring, your enthusiasm is infectious and your commitment to our readers is the foundation of our success.

Dad, as with everything I take on in life, your unwavering support and sage advice has enabled me to accomplish yet another dream. Thank you for always thinking of me.

The Penguins – thank you for believing in me and my vision, for valuing my words and ideas, and for seeing my potential to impact others. I am so appreciative of every single person who made this book possible, and so honoured to represent your organization. A big warm hug to Cate – thank you for championing us, for trusting us and for all your love and enthusiasm. Loryn and I look forward to many more a rosé! To the talented Grace – I so appreciate you really listening to our vision and bringing it to life perfectly. This book is everything I imagined it to be! Christine – thank you for polishing me perfectly while allowing my voice to shine. What an effortless dream team we were. And to Lou, my soul sister, you are just the best!

The AA dream team – Sally, John, Pauline, Loryn, Ellen and Janene. I so respect each of you for your passion, enthusiasm and commitment to our customers, our quality and our integrity. My achievements are your achievements and I couldn't think of brighter people to share my days with. Oysters and champagne to celebrate!

Big hugs to all my friends, cheerleaders and allies – you energize and propel me forward with your belief and backing. An incredibly special thanks to the Booth family. For the past sixteen years you have consistently been the most wonderful and loving support, and with this book you've taken it to the next level. Your beautiful home was an absolute dream and completed these pages perfectly – thank you thank you! To one Booth in particular, couldn't do life without you. And a special shout-out to my biggest cheerleader Craig: you are a ray of sunshine and forever an adopted member of the family. Your enthusiasm for everything we do means more to me than you know.

Finally, thank you to every single customer who has bought one of my eight books. It is my privilege to share my ideas with you and it is my honour to have a place on your bookshelf. And to you reading this, thank you for trusting me on your thermo journey – it is my goal to add value and for my recipes and ideas to enrich your life.

Eight books later I still leave the acknowledgements to write last, and I still get a little teary as I write them!

DIETARY REQUIREMENTS RECIPE LISTS

DAIRY FREE RECIPES

aioli, egg-free 45
almond and garlic spread 43
apple rhubarb breakfast crumble 227
apple sauerkraut, smoky 57
banana breads, mini spelt 87
beetroot, 'canned' 141
bread rolls, basic 211
breakfast beans 219
broccoli poke bowl 31
carrot cake 207
cauliflower pizza bases 17
chilli con lentil 147
chilli oil 37
cinnamon raisin bagels 195
coconut seed chews 75
creamy cauliflower soup 183
dirty burgers 157
dukkah, classic 35
falafels 15
fermented flavour bomb paste 63
free-form summer fruit tart 99
friendly frosting 212
garlic crumbs 41
green curry paste 161
harissa eggplant dip 85
hot choccy, Ellen's 225
kombucha 55
lemon tart, Loryn's 91
mango sorbet, scoopable 97
marshmallows, raspberry 103
Mexican brisket 155
mustard dressing, zingy 47
oats, loaded 217
olive bread, foolproof 205
one-bowl tomato spaghetti 23
onion jam, too easy 135
passionfruit margarita, frozen 115
peanut dipping sauce 49
pears, vanilla poached 229
pho, Loryn's flavourful 247
piccalilli, Pauline's 137

pina colada snow cones 101
pine-lime watermelon pops 105
plum paste 131
potato gnocchi 171
potatoes, crispy spiced 191
pumpkin curry 145
quinoa veggie soup, nourishing 239
rainbow rice 29
red curry paste 163
rhubarb cordial 133
rice + veggie bake 241
rye fruit bread, mum's 209
salted caramel bliss balls 77
seed bark 79
sesame mayo 51
smoothie bowl, tropical green 113
spaghetti bolognaise 175
spiced apple cake 199
spring green pasta 25
spring salad with miso dressing 27
sweet seed sprinkles 39
Thai chilli oysters 21
Thai red lentil soup 153
Thai zucchini soup 13
tomato passata 129
turmeric elixir 119
vegetable bolognaise 151
veggie gyoza 159
watermelon crush 117

DAIRY FREE OPTION RECIPES

brown rice risotto, 'the' 245
creamy pasta, easy 237
fruit jellies 81
ice cream, easy 93
mushroom sausage rolls, mini 185

GLUTEN FREE RECIPES

GLUTEN FREE OPTION RECIPES

VEGETARIAN RECIPES

aioli, egg-free 47
almond and garlic spread 43
apple pie with flaky pastry 201
apple rhubarb breakfast crumble 227
apple sauerkraut, smoky 57
banana breads, mini spelt 87
beetroot, 'canned' 141
bread rolls, basic 211
broccoli poke bowl 31
brown rice risotto, 'the' 245
carrot cake 207
cauliflower pizza bases 17
chilli con lentil 147
chilli oil 37
cinnamon raisin bagels 195
coconut seed chews 75
creamy cauliflower soup 183
creamy pasta, easy 237
dirty burgers 157
dukkah, classic 35
falafels 15
fermented flavour bomb paste 63
free-form summer fruit tart 99
friendly frosting 212
garlic crumbed sprouts 189
garlic crumbs 41
gingerbread spelt cookies 197
green curry paste 161
harissa eggplant dip 85
hot choccy, Ellen's 225
ice cream, easy 93
kombucha 55
lemon tart, Loryn's 91
lemonade, probiotic 61
mango sorbet, scoopable 97
maple cream cheese frosting 213
mushroom sausage rolls, mini 185
mustard dressing, zingy 47
oats, loaded 217
olive bread, foolproof 205
one-bowl tomato spaghetti 23
onion jam, too easy 135

pancakes, fluffy 221
passionfruit margarita, frozen 115
peanut dipping sauce 49
pears, vanilla poached 229
pho, Loryn's flavourful 247
piccalilli, Pauline's 137
pina colada snow cones 101
pine-lime watermelon pops 105
pizza 243
plum paste 131
polenta pizza 179
potato gnocchi 171
potatoes, crispy spiced 191
pumpkin curry 145
quinoa veggie soup, nourishing 239
rainbow rice 29
red curry paste 163
rhubarb cordial 133
rice + veggie bake 241
rough puff tart 235
rye fruit bread, mum's 209
salted caramel bliss balls 77
seed bark 79
sesame mayo 51
simple summer tarts 83
smoothie bowl, tropical green 113
spanakopita cigars 19
spiced apple cake 199
spring green pasta 25
sweet seed sprinkles 39
Thai red lentil soup 153
Thai zucchini soup 13
tomato passata 129
turmeric elixir 119
vegetable bolognaise 151
veggie gyoza 159
watermelon crush 117
yoghurt, super thick 59

VEGETARIAN OPTION RECIPES

breakfast beans 219

VEGAN RECIPES

VEGAN OPTION RECIPES

The secret ingredient
is always love.

INDEX

VIKING

UK | USA | Canada | Australia
India | New Zealand | South Africa | China

Penguin Books is part of the Penguin Random House group of companies
whose addresses can be found at global.penguinrandomhouse.com.

Penguin
Random House
Australia

First published by Penguin Random House Australia Pty Ltd, 2018

Photographer and food stylist: Loryn Babauskis
Designer: Grace West
Editor: Christine Osmond

Printed and bound in China by 1010 Printing International Ltd

A catalogue record for this
book is available from the
National Library of Australia

Hardback ISBN 978 0 14379 441 7
Paperback ISBN 978 0 14378 923 9

penguin.com.au